Louise's Leaves

By Louise Frazier

DEDICATION:

To Biodynamic and Organic growers whose toil as pioneers in the frontier of today's sustainable agriculture may yet lead us to sound the trumpets of Jerico.

In grateful acknowledgement for the contributions of:

Wolfgang Rohrs

Brian T. Fitzgerald

Sarah Simmons

friends and family

whose interest, support and assistance made this work possible.

P.O. Box 550

Kimberton, PA 19442

ISBN 0-938250-50-7

Printed in U.S.A.

Book Design: Sandra Gargus

Illustrations: Wolfgang Rohrs

Introduction

Although these "Leaves" were originally conceived with the encouragement of a friend in Buffalo, New York during the Winter of the blizzard of '85, I actually began writing them 5 years later. while living on Sunways Biodynamic CSA* Farm in Housatonic, Massachusetts. Share members were unfamiliar with some of the wide variety of vegetables they received in their share each week and were in a quandary about what to do when a crop came in abundance. At the request of the gardener, I wrote some "Leaves" to put in the weekly shares, giving tidbits of information and tips on preparing the vegetables in question. We hoped they would assist those creating meals from the vegetables, as well as deepen interest in the fare offered in every season from the farm.

They are the result of over 12 years of experiences Wolfgang and I have had in maintaining a fulfilling diet based largely on food from local farms using sustainable agricultural practices, both in the U.S. and Europe.

In the early 1980's, we opened a vegetarian restaurant, with 3 other partners, in Cologne, Germany with a menu based on produce delivered to our door from local and regional Biodynamic and organic farms. We became expert at pleasing the taste-buds of our customers, even when faced with a large delivery of pumpkins that had to be used that week or in Winter when we were dependent upon root crops, cabbages and hardy greens for fare. Rather than limiting us, these situations challenged our creativity, leading to some unusual and delicious dishes. We learned a great deal from visiting the growers who supplied our produce. As we walked their fields and talked with them, our understanding of different vegetables was broadened, adding to our sensitivity in preparing and combining them into tasty, wholesome dishes.

Later in the U.S. it took a while before we could find others who shared our enthusiasm in this direction here. Fortunately we did find some sharing these interests in the food cooperatives and natural food stores wherever we lived. Then at Sunways, we became fully engaged in all the questions facing a developing farm intending to sustain itself while providing members in

Introduction *(Continued)*

the community with healthy food through all the seasons—from the health of the soil and the environment, to the livelihood of those tending the soil, the overall financial sustainability of the farm, and ultimately to the well-being of the local community.

For us it is clear that local Biodynamic® and organically grown seasonal fare has its importance in coming to a harmonious relationship with our environment wherever we find ourselves. North, South, East or West, in varying degrees every region has its seasons and foods that nourish and help us to thrive there. It has been our observation that in a temperate climate we feel warmer and healthier in cold Winter weather when using roots and other locally grown storage vegetables, and more comfortable in Summer, and the transition seasons of Spring and Fall, when dependent on the produce nature bestows on us through local growers working the land with Biodynamic and organic practices.

Completing the 52 "Leaves" for all four seasons, while living in northern Vermont for the past two years, has further served to confirm our convictions. We have been supplied with the full range of vegetables contained herein by a local organic grower, with whom we have exchanged concurring ideas. On a recent early Winter visit to Florida, we adapted quickly to the warm weather by preparing locally-grown organic foods, based on our late-Spring and early Summer "Leaves". Within a few days of our return to northern cold and snow, we again could maintain ourselves in good health with warming root vegetable stews and soups. In both cases, we felt akin to the local natural environment as well.

Using the "Leaves" as a guide should be possible even in more southern or northern regions by following what is coming from local farms and referring to the index. Most people living in the temperate zones will find the book applicable as presented. Others may find they can follow the entries within a week or two as given. In any case, it is hoped that you will find eating with the seasons in your area a tasty, enlivening experience.

—Louise Frazier

*Community Supported Agriculture

MAY

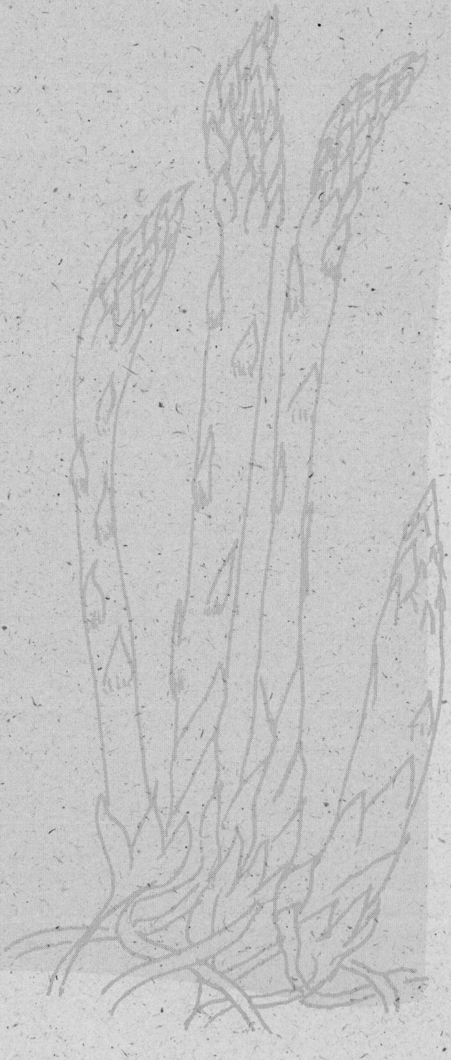

May's 1st Week

Spinach! Spinach! Spinach!

Welcome a new season of abundance with Spring's emerald green spinach, so easily prepared into various dishes to please the palates of one and all. Originating as a wild vegetable in the Caucasian area of the Middle East, it was brought to Europe in the 16th Century. Cultivated widely since then, it has been recognized as high in chlorophyll, vitamins and minerals, almost to the point of mythology.

The younger, freshly harvested leaves are tasty even to finicky eaters, lowest in oxalic acid, and are best for those with sensitivities such as gout. Please be sure to select only organically grown spinach, as chemical fertilizers tend to produce leaves containing high levels of nitrates.

Spinach carries the sand or soil in which it grows on leaf and stems, so it may require more than one **swish-wash** bath in deep water. The rule is to wash until water appears clear. For salads or storage, drain or **spin off** excess water. To store, wrap leaves in a damp towel, refrigerate for later use.

Spinach **should not** be subjected to heat for more than a few minutes—only until bright green in color—and should NEVER BE REHEATED! Long cooking develops its oxalic acid content into an intolerable form that is best avoided by everyone.

Fold **lightly steamed** or **sauteed** seasoned spinach into **crepes**, or layer between thin pancakes—pour cheese, tofu or spaghetti sauce over. **Puree** spinach for creamed soup or sauce. **Add fresh chopped spinach** last minute to soups or pasta prima vera—or enjoy spinach simply cooked as a dinner vegetable—a few of the many recipes available world-wide.

Chives, dill, oregano, nutmeg or allspice are **complements** to spinach—thyme too, at times. Dill especially enhances a **delicious salad dressing** made by finely mincing 1/2 lb of fresh spinach leaves and blending with juice of a lemon, 2 Tbs tamari (or herb salt to taste), 1 Tbs dried dill weed (or 4 Tbs of chopped fresh dill) and 1/2C of light oil. Mix with grains—rice, rye or buckwheat/kasha—for hearty salad.

Of course a bowl of fresh spinach leaf salad is delectable—by itself or **tossed** with other greens, chives, slices of radish, tangerine or apple in season. **Sprinkle** with toasted sesame seeds for a bacony flavor.

Notes

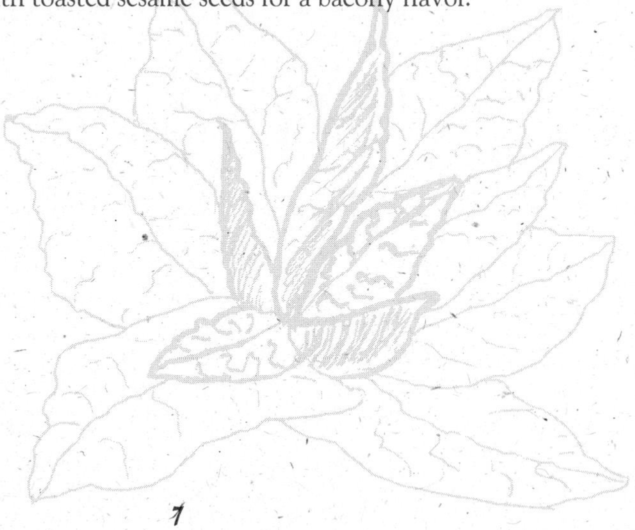

May's 2nd Week

Garden Greens

The early delicate leaf lettuces, the young lacy Japanese mustard green, Mizuna, and the baby Oriental "choys" with white succulent stems and deep green unfurling leaf-tops come to us now from local growers. They are part of the lush green wave rapidly spreading over field and meadow, basking in the sun and filling with vitamins and minerals.

Delightful bowls of leafy green salads once again enhance daily menus. Simply swish-wash, drain or spin, and tear or snip the greens into bite-sized pieces. The baby leaves can be kept whole. We find that serving whole large leafs can be awkward to eat, and sometimes cause messy splattering of dressing, cutting them on salad plate or in bowl at the table just doesn't work well.

Tossed together, the different varieties complement each other in taste and texture. Sprinkle with chive snips and dress with a light **Spring lemon juice based dressing**—dill weed, tarragon or dried mustard are good seasoning choices as well as a little herb salt.

Serve green leafy salads as an accompaniment to any meal or as the **entree** itself, adding chopped nuts, pumpkin or sunflower seeds, cheese—grated or crumbled such as feta. Tiny toasted whole grain bread **croutons** tossed in, a slice of fresh whole grain bread on the side or chips & crackers add satisfying goodness to a salad meal.

Also nice to serve with a green salad is a **protein-rich spread** for bread or crackers. A similar dip for chips serves nicely as well. Walnuts, lentils, hummus, and herbed cottage or curd type cheese make a good base for spread. **Stuff** a good sized portion of this salad into a whole grain pita for a delicious meal in a pocket!

When the stems of the greens—especially Mizuna—are longer, they can be **sliced into little rings** and added to pasta or grain salads. The stems of the Choys are good in green salad too. Slice them on a slight diagonal into **ribbons** and toss in.

As for left-over dressed salad, chill and use soon in another dish. Lightly **saute** and fold into crepes or omelettes; blend and add to soups; or blend and use as a base for a cold **Gazpacho-type** soup.

Notes

May's 3rd Week

Rhubarb

With all the exuberance of green, a blush appears in the garden. It is first noticeable on the stems of rhubarb, a member of the herbaceous leaf family (knotgrass) that also includes buckwheat and sorrel. Cultivated for over 4000 years in the Orient from a variety growing wild in the Himalayas, rhubarb spread from southern Russia to the Mediterranean and then all over Europe, where it was enjoyed in many recipes as a Spring cure.

Rich in Vitamin A, C, & minerals, rhubarb is said to revitalize the blood, bring digestion to order, and spark the appetites of lackluster children. Only the stems of rhubarb are edible, and soon after the leaf appears, its daily growth is noticeable. The leaves are TOXIC and inedible for humans! Later these toxins go into the stem. Rhubarb season ends by July.

Beyond pie—best known of all—are many other delicious and interesting ways to serve rhubarb (contrary to the claims of many unaware of other delights). The tartness in rhubarb develops as it grows, so use the slender young stems to **serve raw**.

Simply wash young fresh rhubarb stems, slice in ringlets and **mix into grain, leafy or other Spring salads—even in potato**! Spark up breakfast by adding some crisp slightly tart ringlets to Muesli or cereal. We like it in our **Muesli** with finely grated carrots and raisins or other dried fruit.

Small rhubarb slices are good in Spring soups. Add the last few minutes of cooking to maintain their texture and taste. Use instead of lemon juice and rind in April's Spring Tonic recipe. Also complements spinach soup.

When **turnips and peas** arrive on the scene, add small cuts of rhubarb when cooking them—add later so as not to lose their flavor by overcooking. Similarly tasty with **prima vera**. Season these dishes with dill or thyme.

For **dessert**, try a cornmeal rhubarb pudding. Soak 1/2C of cornmeal mixed with 1/2C water and 1C apple or white grape juice for 30 min. in a pot. Stir in 1 lb rhubarb cut into 1/4-1/2" thick slices; bring slowly to boil; simmer a bit—stirring—until cornmeal thickens, but rhubarb holds its shape. Cool 10 min; add a little nutmeg or mace, 1/2 tsp vanilla, and optional sweetening: honey, maple syrup, raisins or chopped organic banana. Chill and serve.

Notes

May's 4th Week

Asparagus

Along with its other lily family members, asparagus shoots up its green stalks in Spring, whereupon it is eaten for a few weeks in its budding state. Later it flowers into a large lacy fern. Asparagus was evident in ancient Egypt and Greece. Later, Plato and then Caesar expressed their delight in eating it.

From earliest times, it was considered medicinal—a view still held by some today, who avoid or limit its use as a food. In Spring cures asparagus has been highly valued for its diuretic qualities, as well as for its high mineral and rutin content.

In Europe, garden asparagus is covered with soil to keep it white until harvested. This is not usual practice here where we enjoy it sun-grown and deep-green. It can be served either **fresh and raw** in a variety of salads or **lightly cooked** for **vegetable, entree or soup**.

It is best to wash asparagus quickly and stand heads-up to drain. To serve the tenderest part, break off the bottom at the point where it snaps away easily, and use the remaining top. It may be possible to use a bit more of the bottom portion by slicing from snap point until knife no longer cuts easily, indicating woodiness, which should be discarded. These tender bottom slices can be used for **soup**.

Ideally asparagus is **steamed standing upright** on its stems with the heads just under the lid of the pot. Another way is to place a long, fatter asparagus at the edge of a shallow pan and lay heads of the rest on this one, out of fluid. **Simmer** a few minutes in very little water until bright green and tips are firm but yielding when pressed between the fingers. A dash of nutmeg, dill, tarragon or chervil may be sprinkled on the stalks, and after cooking, a little salt—or reserve the seasoning for a sauce.

Make a **tofu Hollandaise** by blending 1C tofu, juice of one and a half lemons, 1/2C light oil, tamari or herb salt to taste and choice of above seasonings. A pinch of white pepper or dry mustard can add a bit of zip. Heat on low or in a double boiler. Much less rich than original Hollandaise! Or instead, try a dollop of **herbed room-temperature yoghurt** or add a blend of lemon juice, water, seasonings and arrowroot to **pan juices for sauce**.

Notes

Broccoli

It is in this century that Broccoli has become popular as a vegetable and we find it on menus ringing the globe. A member of the cabbage family which—like cauliflower—has developed into a flowering state, broccoli is packed with the health-giving nutrients its deep-green color signifies.

Care in maintaining this green color from garden to table is necessary to assure its benefits and good flavor. Also important to note is that broccoli, as cauliflower, is best NEVER EATEN RAW! They both contain a toxin against their predators which is dispelled through heating.

For **dips and salads**, cut to size desired and **blanch** in boiling-hot water for a minute or so. Cool at once with a dip in icy cold water. Drain and serve—or chill for later.

Quick cooking in any case is ideal for broccoli, either by **stir-fry** or **steaming**. The florettes need little cooking, while the stems require a bit more time, but should still be crisp and green. Heads up and stems down in cooking! When combining with other vegetables, add broccoli in the last few minutes of cooking. Leaves are also edible.

To clean, soak broccoli—heads down—in cold salted water (1tsp salt to 1/2 gallon) for 5 min. Hidden predators clinging in the florettes detach themselves to get away from the salt and float upwards. This process avoids the embarrassment of one appearing later on the plate—which was the case in our restaurant when the preparer felt disinclined to salt-soak.

As with asparagus, cut off and discard the bottom of the broccoli stem at the point where it becomes woody. Peel the stem if skin seems thick, but center is crisp. **Slice** all the way up the stem, for dishes like stir-fry and prima vera or for soups, trimming or breaking off small florettes.

Cook broccoli with a sprinkling of caraway, dill or such seeds to **aid digestion**. Season further with oregano, dill, curry, or ginger to complement dish being served.

Broccoli raab or "Calabrese" in Italian, whether gathered wild or cultivated, is another tasty form beloved by many in Europe. It grows like flowers, on leafy stalks with tiny florettes here and there. Chop and cook like kale or make into a **delicious soup** cooking with onions and cornmeal or millet in a broth.

Notes

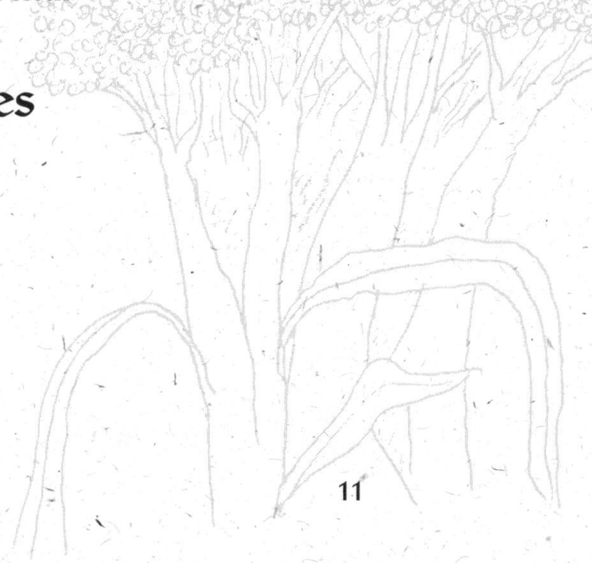

Edible Flowers

"Gather ye flowers while you may!" For a few short months, edible varieties from woodlands, field and garden entice the senses in bouquets and garnishes at the table. Containing the heightened qualities of a plant, edible flowers delight with their sweet or snappy bite. Served fresh, they gaily garnish our food and are rarely heated—squash blossoms and day lily buds being exceptions.

Have no fear for harming flowers when biting into them. They are at the peak of life and reach fulfillment when releasing their essences—into the air or the mouth. A variety of flowers await our enjoyment.

White and purple violets blink colorfully when strewn on a tossed green salad. Their nectar is cupped where blossom joins stem, and sweetly bursts when bitten.

Likewise, flowers on herbs are delicious—in **salads**, as a fresh garnish on a dish containing the herb leaf or afloat on top of a cup of Summer vegetable **broth**.

Nasturtiums come into our kitchen with leaves like cool green fans or water lily pads and brightly colored flowers that bring us a sense of the Sun. There is a **hint of pepper** in their taste, combining coolness and subtle spice for a lift in Summer. It is said they possess anti-biotic qualities. Toss bite-size nasturtium leaves with salad greens or line the salad bowl with the larger leaves. Place the flowers on top to delight the eye as well as the taste buds. Guaranteed to perk everyone up! Nasturtiums and cucumbers are complementary too—nice as a salad or in **Summer sandwiches**.

Sprinkle **rose petals** on salads—vegetable or fruit. A jar of rose petals and water steeped in the Sun make a **light refreshing tea**. Lifter of the spirit and comforter in stress, even as a garnish, the aromatic rose is an **elixir** for the heart of children and adults.

Borage blossoms bring courage—their leaves as well. Serve fresh in salads or **cold drinks**; float atop punch.

In Japan, **chrysanthemum petals** are served with hot broth. In China the flowers are used in **teas** for calmness and clarity of vision. **Linden flowers** are similarly used in Europe.

Notes

JUNE

June's 1st Week

Radishes

Spring's blush turns to red in the radish—signaling the approach of colorful Summer! Crisp and snappy tasting, bunches of bright-red globe radishes are usually first to appear on the scene—and welcome they are. They leap out in stark contrast amongst all the proliferating greens, whose season they now share.

Most folks are sparked to rinse and enjoy them out-of-hand. Some like to dash them with salt. Beware: too much salt can cause the radish to feel like lead in the stomach. Otherwise they are an excellent aid to digestion. For those with sensitive systems, coarsely-grated radishes are best. It's a nice way to prepare them for tossed salads too, besides thinly sliced.

Do try to prepare radishes **just before serving**, thereby preserving all their goodness. Washing can be done ahead and then they can be kept whole, **damp-wrapped** and refrigerated until ready for use.

Don't discard those **radish tops**! I still remember my surprise when finding Salad Nicoise served in Nice with a whole red radish on top—leafy greens still attached. A sense of lushness brimmed out of that salad bowl. Not knowing what to do, I soon joined the experienced in eating bulb and leaf **au-naturel**: delightful!

We wash the tops and consider them as another green to be **snipped into salads** or to **garnish** soups and entrees. What we can't use we put in our **stock crock**—composting wilted and excess.

Europeans serve **grated radish on whole grain bread** for breakfast, as well as later for lunch. As with food in general, they feel it best to eat more early in the day, and little if any radish with the evening meal. Radishes are valued highly as a cure, especially for those with **liver or gall bladder** problems. More recently radishes have been found to be helpful against the **skin eruptions** of herpes, acne and boils.

Radishes are rich in **calcium**, along with other minerals—including sulphur held in their mustard oil—and are noted for their cleansing qualities. A little eaten daily is recommended, especially for elders. Large amounts once in a while don't contribute towards healing, but certainly give pleasure!

Notes

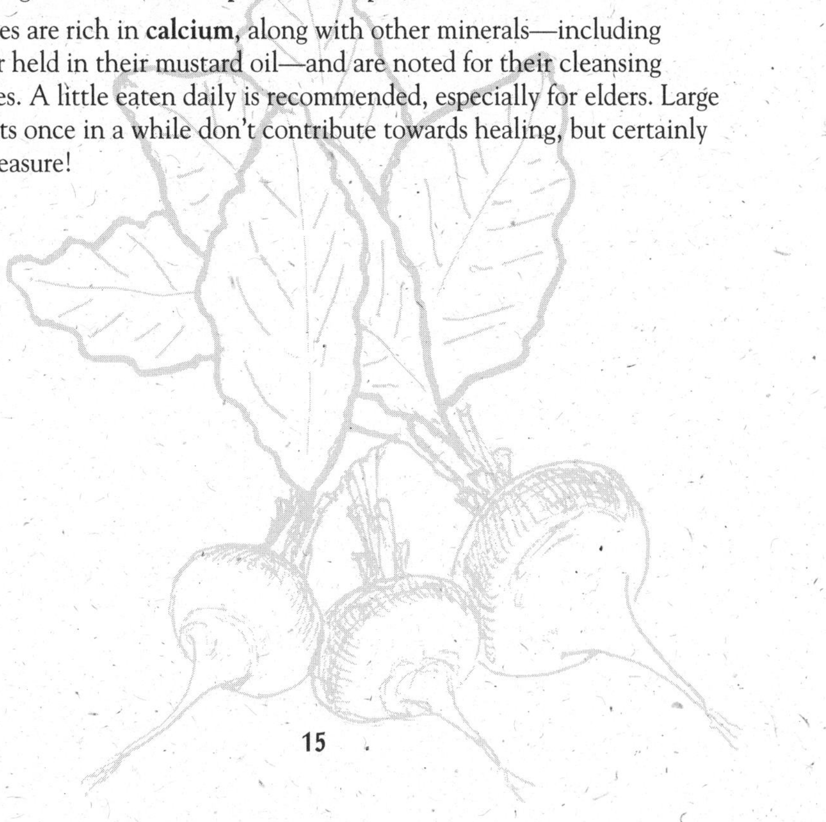

Peas

Snow, sugar snap and shell peas are on their way! First come the succulent edible pod types containing tiny peas or nubbins—in the case of snow peas. The latter have come to us from the Orient and are particularly delicious in stir-fry dishes.

The sugar snap variety looks like a small shell pea, but please never shell these babies! Their shells are juicy, crisp and easily snapped into bite sized pieces, while the younger ones can be served whole.

Both snow and snap peas sweetly flesh out our fare as we proceed towards the summer season. They are a delight to the palette as we move away from the strong, bitter herbs and greens of Spring. Their ease of preparation is appealing to the cook as well.

Simply snip off the stem end—a kitchen shears does nicely here—and rinse under cold water. Serve them **fresh or blanched** for salads, whole or snipped smaller. As they grow larger, a string may develop along one side, in which case **cutting across** the pod renders them chewable.

Edible pod-peas can be **tossed** with green salads, cut up and added to grain salads, or **marinated** alone or with other vegetables. They are superb with scallions and dill fronds.

To serve hot, **lightly stir-fry** in oil 2 - 3 minutes until bright green; or steam them whole or in cuts. Delicious with broccoli, asparagus and new white turnips. **Float** cuts in brothy soups, adding them a few minutes before serving. Dill seed and weed/fronds, chervil or nutmeg are all good seasonings for peas.

Peas have a high protein content, the more so as they develop and become larger—like shell peas, which can be used for protein **with grains**. Nice with rice, buckwheat, millet and pasta—especially Prima Vera style—or added to potato dishes.

Shell peas are legumes and **require cooking/blanching** to bring them from a protein-inhibiting state into an assimilable food. Besides including them in vegetable soup, try a pureed soup of freshly cooked peas. In hot weather, **add mint** for coolness & digestibility—tasty chilled too!

Notes

June's 3rd Week

Turnips & Kohlrabi

Now the gardens flesh out further, yielding baby pearl white turnips and pale green kohlrabi. They are members of the Brassica family and are highly valued today for their preventive and health-giving qualities.

They can be prepared in similar ways for enjoying their delicate new-season flavors. In addition to the bulb, the green leaves can be used in salads, soups, and vegetable pots. As with other greens, they need only light cooking.

The white turnip pearls make a jewel of a soup. Simmer whole, if small, or cut-up if larger, with scallion rings and fennel or dill seeds for flavor and digestion. When just fork-tender, add chopped green leafy tops; coriander, basil or dill weed with salt to taste; and vegetable or miso broth. Heat to piping hot and serve in bowls with grated or sliced radishes. Chopped parsley is good too.

Kohlrabi makes a pale jade kohlslaw that is refreshing to the eye as well as the palette. Simply wash—peel skin only if it seems tough—medium grate and toss with your favorite dressing. For complements, add your choice of grated radish, chopped parsley, snips of green onion, dill and/or basil.

Prepare a hot dish of kohlrabi and/or white turnips, by steaming or simmering, in a similar fashion as the soup above. Add a little lemon juice to the pot and no broth. When vegetables are tender crisp, remove to serving dish and thicken pot juices with arrowroot powder dissolved in water (1 Tbs of arrowroot to 1C of fluid generally makes for sauce consistency.) Season as for soup. For a bit of sharpness, add a little dried mustard at the end with the thickening. Garnish with radish and parsley.

Serve millet, rice or buckwheat with kohlrabi and turnips. The addition of cooked millet or rice will turn a soup recipe into more filling fare—a good use of leftover grains. The short time required to cook either of these vegetables in not enough to cook them with the grains.

Larger kohlrabi are delicious stuffed. Scoop out the center, saving it for slaw or soup. Fill with a mixture of onion, parsley, herbs and oat flakes, bread crumbs or cooked grain. Simmer in a covered pan about 20 mins.

Notes

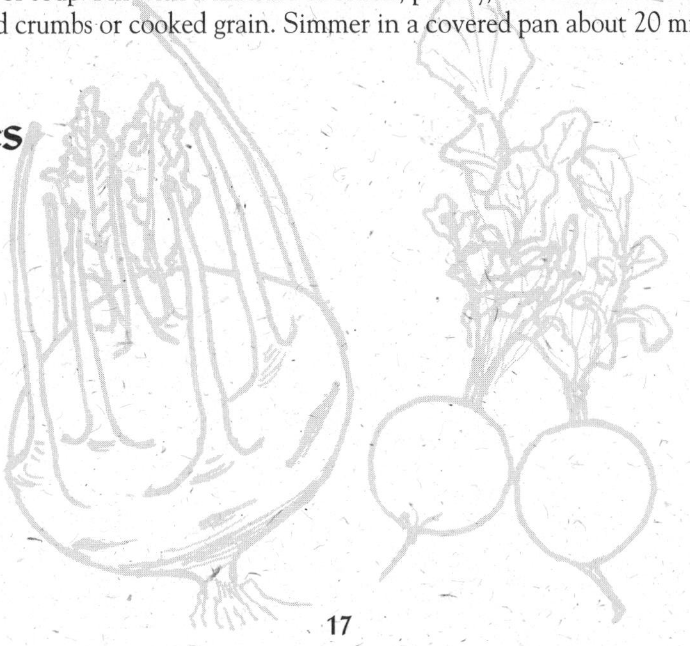

June's 4th Week

The Herbs Are Coming!

Now we begin to find bouquets of aromatic fresh green herbs in the market place—just in time to enliven our Summer fare! Any vegetable can be served frequently and still be welcome at the table simply by varying the herbs that flavor it. A boon when bumper crops appear!

- **Summer Savory** complements early cabbage. Try some of its fine, narrow leaves fresh in **slaw**; chop stems for cooked recipes; add long stems with leaves to soup pot and remove after cooking. Savory's also good with Swiss Chard, eggplant and beans. **It aids digestion.** Use in place of allspice, pepper or mint in Summer recipes.
- **Tarragon** subtly flavors cabbage, asparagus, cucumbers and lettuce. Known in France as one of the "Fine Herbs", along with chervil, parsley and thyme. Combines nicely with dill or fennel.
- **Dill** is ever popular with its aroma and light pickle flavor. **Sprinkled** on asparagus, string beans, peas, salads and all the brassicas—among others—dill cheers the appetite! At its best harvested just before its yellow blossoms open.
- **Oregano** is famous in pizza and other Italian dishes. It's a bit peppery when fresh—use sparingly to **spark salads**! It enhances broccoli, green beans, spinach, the summer squashes, peppers and Mediterranean or Mexican cookery.
- And ah, **Sweet Basil**! Remarkable in salads, tremendous with tomatoes and summer squashes, a favorite minced into **pesto**, basil keeps flies away. Its cool qualities grace a myriad of dishes all around the Mediterranean. Toss bite-sized leaves into green **salads**; snip fresh into zucchini slaw or **pancakes**; add lots of whole leaves last minute to ratatouille. Chop basil with stems for **soups**. Combine basil with savory to pep up spirits on hot, humid days.
- Gaining in popularity is **Cilantro**—the pungent herb of the coriander plant. Long used in Peruvian dishes, but until recently considered only a bug-chaser in Western cultures, it is at home with Indian curries and Tex-Mex fare. Folks are either delighted or distanced by exotic cilantro!

Refrigerate fresh green herbs in a jar, stems down, in an inch of water, with a plastic bag over the leafy tops.

Notes

JULY

July's 1st Week

New Roots

Red beets make their Summer debut! Vibrant color dashes on stage—like a 4th of July celebration. In their early juicy-crisp state, beets have tender thin skins and need only be washed to remove soil. Their trace minerals, so vital to us, reside just under the skin, so scrub if covered with soil, but don't peel away all that goodness!

Treat tossed salads to some red-veined green leaves of Summer beet tops. They are also delicious cooked in place of spinach—just as that crop fades with Summer's heat.

Beets are excellent finely **grated** and served fresh. Cup some in a green leaf—either beet top or lettuce—for each serving. Sprinkle with **lemon juice and dill**; cap with a few **blueberries** or black **raspberries**; top with grated radish. Make a platter full for red, white and blue cheers!

If you prefer, toss finely-grated fresh new beets with lots of luscious greens, along with the blueberries or black raspberries. Add a lemon juice, oil and dill dressing and top with the radishes—grated or thin sliced.

Ladle chilled **puree** of fresh beet and cucumber soup, seasoned with fresh tarragon or basil over red or black raspberries. Adds a delightful tart bite midst the sweetness of beets.

Looking for a more substantial salad? Wash and puree 1 lb of fresh new beets; add the juice of 1 to 2 lemons, herbs—basil or dill—and tamari or salt to taste; blend well with 1/4C of light oil. Mix this thick colorful dressing with **cool, cooked grains** such as rice or buckwheat, along with green onion snips. A nice alternative to macaroni or potato salad.

Substitute new fresh **baby carrots** for beets in the above recipes. They'll be coming from the garden in a week or two, adding orange to Nature's vibrant palette of Summer colors. In place of berries, slices of fresh organic apricots, peaches, pineapple or citrus complement carrots in summer—as do cilantro or basil, altogether too.

Don't discard all the **carrot tops**! Like beet greens, they contain vital nutrients. Snip a little into salads, soups or dishes with cooked carrots. Put some in the stock pot, but don't overwhelm the pot with their strength.

Notes

Summer Squashes

Abundance comes into our midst with the yellow, white and green squashes of Summer. Tender crookneck is followed by the round scalloped patty pan variety, while zucchini begins its annual proliferation. From warmth-loving vines these succulent vegetables blossom forth to nourish and cool us in the heat of summer.

They can be served freshly sliced for vegetable platters; coarsely grated for garnish, slaw or tossing with greens; and lightly cooked in numerous ways as an entree or side dish. Cook Summer squashes only to the point where they are juicy and still crunchy—delectable!

Fresh basil and Summer squash are a perfect marriage. Add an extra measure of fresh basil to cooked recipes like ratatouille, stirring in as cooking finishes to maintain its cool green flavor. Ratatouille comes to us from the French Provence and is a **stew** in which the cook combines other vegetables of the season with lots of Summer squash.

Fresh oregano in small measure adds a peppery bite to squash dishes. Dill holds its own charm lending a piquant flavor, especially tasty in fresh squash salads or in a **sauce** for patty pan and spaghetti squash (when the latter comes in towards Summer's end). Herbs are one way to **bring variety** into preparing numerous dishes from abundant squash. Others are to mix or match them as below.

Zucchini certainly calls for creativity in the kitchen, if we are to take advantage of its bounty and continue to please partakers. For starters try **zucchini pancakes**—made like potato pancakes—or lightly saute zucchini with herbs. Next time add green onions, then sweet peppers. **Simmer** them all together early in the season with peas, later with celery, tomatoes and eggplant for ratatouille.

Zucchini as a **soup** with fresh dill or added to other vegetables, macaroni and chick peas for minestrone are ideas for a rainy day. If the rain keeps up, consider **zucchini "boats"**—lengthwise halved larger zucchini, centers scooped out and filled with a grain/vegetable mixture (millet is nice), and baked topped with cheese, sesame or sunflower seeds.

Grill thick lengthwise-sliced squash brushed with salad dressing—a hit over the coals when cooking out!

Notes

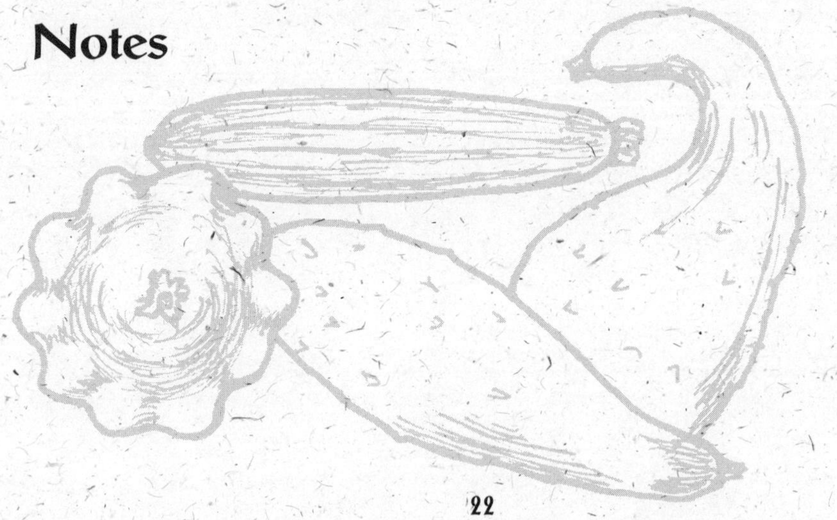

July's 3rd Week

Cool Cucumbers

Cucumbers have a long history—over 4000 years—and are noted for improving the complexion, cleansing the liver, aiding in digestion, diabetes, and headaches, as well as helping us to keep "cool as a cucumber" in Summer.

The long green "cuke" that grows fatter on the vine is most familiar to us, with the smaller gherkin-type a close second. The latter is usually preserved as a pickle, but it is also tasty fresh at the table.

Recent to our scene is the long, thinner European ridged cucumber, with less seeds and a tender smooth skin—nice for slicing. Pale yellow round lemon cucumbers have been showing up lately too. Delicate of skin, they have a hint-of-lemon flavor and are delicious simply **cut into quarters or small wedges**. Eat as is or sprinkle with fresh dill.

As with radishes, salt makes cucumbers harder to digest, so if you're looking for **more flavor**, splash with a little lemon juice instead. Basil and mint combine nicely to enhance cucumbers, or each can be used solo. The flavor of tarragon is appealing too, either fresh or in vinegar, and let's not forget the peppery spike nasturtiums give.

The skins on our traditional green cukes are a bit thicker than the new varieties, so before slicing run a fork down the surface lengthwise piercing through the skin. Not only makes them pleasing to chew, but also looks nice. Try not to peal away all those nutrients lavished under the skin, but if you must peal, do it **lightly** with a peeler—never with a knife! Save the peels and ends in your stock crock for a mineral rich broth.

Chilled soups made with cucumbers can be nourishing and welcome on a hot Summer's day. Coarsely grate and add to chilled vegetable broth along with herbs and a splash of lemon juice—only a dash of salt if you must!

- Make some fresh or dried **pea soup** on a cool day, with chervil or dill as seasoning. Chill some and reserve to serve on a hot day, blended with cucumbers and fresh mint.
- **Puree** fresh beets and cucumbers, season with tarragon, basil or dill. Garnish with berries or stem cherries.

A European favorite is to **braise** seeded, peeled older cucumbers with herbs. Some like to **bake** them, halved and stuffed—like zucchini.

Notes

July's 4th Week

Swiss Chard

Simply called "chard" and revered by my grandmother, it grows sturdy and tall in the garden. Majestically "chard" offers its richness in vitamins and minerals, much as she offered her wisdom and strengths to us. She favored "chard" over spinach for its growing qualities, as well as flavor. Others now share this view in their gardens and kitchens, particularly those wanting to avoid the oxalic acid content of spinach.

Besides the familiar pearly white thick-stemmed variety, a ruby red thinner stemmed Swiss chard is also coming to market from local organic growers. Both types have large, slightly curly green leaves, which can be prepared in much the same ways as spinach.

The leaves make a hearty salad on their own, and can also be mixed with other greens in the bowl. The center rib is a continuation of the sturdy stem and could be a lot to chew if taken in lengthwise. It is best to cut across the leaf, on a diagonal slant, ribbon fashion when preparing it.

Swiss chard is delicious **lightly steamed** or simmered and served as a hot vegetable. Cut the stems on the diagonal into bite-sized pieces and place in the pot first, with whole or cut leaves added on top. Season with savory, nutmeg, marjoram or allspice, and cook quickly, maintaining the bright color of the leaves and crunch of the stems.

In Europe the leaves are cooked alone and the stems are **pickled**, often using the lactic-acid fermentation method that produces sauerkraut. It takes a year, but the results are exquisite—delicate, light, reminiscent of asparagus.

Swiss chard rolled around an herbed millet or buckwheat filling is a dish fit for a king! Choose large leaves, wash in cool water, drain and cut off the stems—reserving them for another dish. CAUTION: exposure to hot water makes chard leaves limp and unable to be handled.

If center rib is thick, cut a notch out of it up into the leaf and make diagonal cross-slits up the rib for pliability. Place **herbed filling** on the leaf, folding and rolling until wrapped. Sunflower seeds or steamed shelled peas can be mixed with the filling for a satisfying entree. Marjoram is tops for seasoning—use an extra measure in the filling and sprinkled some over the rolls. **Simmer** rolls in a covered pan with a little water and lemon juice—mixed with a bit of dried mustard for a spark. Thicken pot juices after cooking for a tasty sauce.

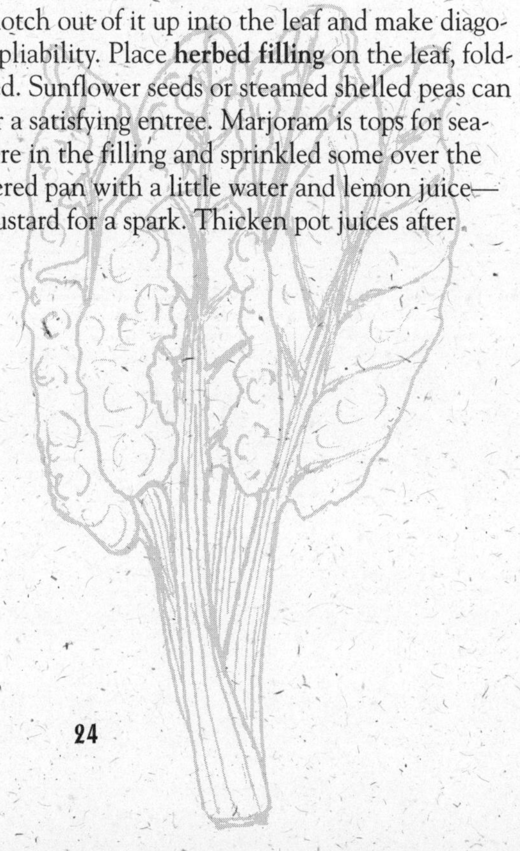

Notes

AUGUST

August's 1st Week

Snap Beans

Along with the green, yellow wax and the more recent appearing deep purple varieties, snap beans are enjoyed for their fleshy, succulent pod. Also called string, bush or pole beans, they have become a favorite garden vegetable. They range in size from the ultra-thin French bean to a wide flat Italian bean of late Summer.

Originating in Chile and brought to Europe for cultivation in the 16th Century, snap beans, have little if any of the high-nitrogen protein content of the sort grown for their developed seed. (The latter have an ancient history and were the type shunned by Pythagoras.) The seeds in snap beans are immature, soft and relatively small by comparison.

Best eaten when young and tender, snap type beans are complemented by dill, oregano, savory, or rosemary. One has to make a choice between preserving color and aroma in preparing fresh garden bean dishes, both among their appealing qualities. **Quick cooking** without a lid produces brilliance of color, while covered cooking intensifies the aroma. Incidentally purple beans turn deep green as soon as they are heated—any disappointment turns to delight with their flavor!

An **old favorite German dish** combines whole green beans, new potatoes, and fresh savory simmered in a covered pot with just enough water to disappear when the vegetables are done. Flavor and aroma are said to be superb! Substitute millet or buckwheat for potatoes for a change.

Snap beans should always be cooked, at least enough to **brighten** the color, but still have a crisp bite. **Crispness** is especially important when serving chilled. Marinating or further cooking lend to **ease in digestibility**, even for more sensitive stomachs.

As **appetizers** or for **picnics**, serve chilled steamed snap beans marinated overnight with onion rings in a dill or rosemary vinaigrette dressing. Chilled herb-steamed beans are also good served whole as a vegetable or tossed with olives in a green salad.

In **Seville green beans**, onions and olives are simmered in water with a little olive oil, strewn with chopped parsley, dashed with black pepper and served hot. For a **tasty Greek dish**, similarly prepare beans with thinly cut strips of fresh peppers, onions, dill and lemon juice.

Notes

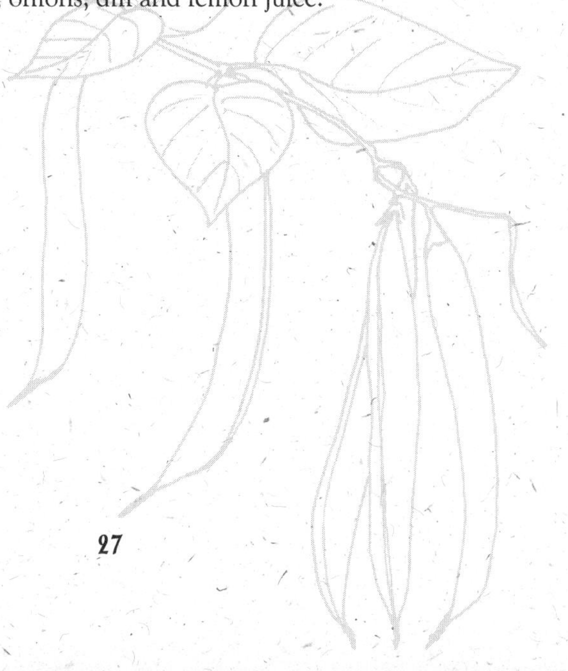

August's 2nd Week

Sweet Corn

There's hardly a soul alive that won't be cheered by being served local, fresh-picked organic corn in the few weeks of its harvest season. It's welcome fare at picnics, buffets or a simple meal at home. Golden, white or mixed; on the cob or off; simmered, grilled or uncooked, fresh sweet corn niblets burst with delight in every bite.

One of the three sisters of life Native Americans taught the new colonists to grow, today's familiar varieties are hybrids of the original "Indian Corn". Ancient strains from South America were small and brightly colored with compact nutritious kernels. While much larger and juicier, our cultivated corn takes many more nutrients from the soil than it returns in health-giving properties.

Fresh cut from the cob, **uncooked** corn niblets are noted, however, as good food for the liver. Delicious as well, young tender fresh niblets add substance and interest to tossed green salads.

- For a **heartier vegetable salad**, mix fresh corn niblets, diced red or green pepper, and sweet onion rings together with lemon juice, oil and herbs—or vinaigrette salad dressing. Marinate for an hour or so before serving. Fresh basil, cilantro, or oregano leaf complement corn salads. Summer squash and ripe tomato cuts are good additions as well.

There are a number of ways to prepare **hot corn-on-the-cob** besides the favorite method of shucking and then submersing in a pot of boiling water for a few minutes. The longer it is cooked, the heavier in carbohydrates corn becomes. It is usually then served with butter and salt.

- For a **lighter version**, add dried leaf thyme or oregano to the water, along with a little oil—tasty as is or with a sprinkle of salt.
- **Grill unshucked ears** over hot, not flaming, charcoal. Some say dip them first in water to prevent drying.
- For **South American style**, shuck only the outer leaves, steam and serve the still encased ears, allowing each person to remove corn leaves and silk just before eating. Enhances aroma, natural flavor and conviviality!

Leftover corn niblets cut from the cob are good added to bean salads, stuffing for vegetables or soups just before serving. Cook older corn niblets in chowders or with zucchini, green beans or other vegetables. For a tasty lunch or supper, make corn fritters. **Bake** niblets in cornmeal muffins too!

Notes

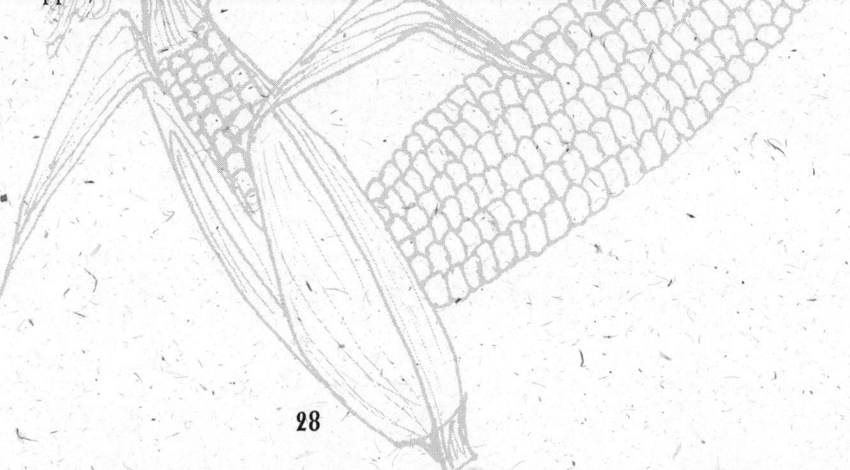

August's 3rd Week

Mediterraneans

From Far East and West, explorers brought vegetables back to the sunny climes of Southern Europe, where they were cradled and cultivated. Various strains emerged and proliferated until they became synonymous with their new homeland. European settlers brought them to the new world and now Mediterranean varieties flourish here.

Eggplant, tomatoes, and peppers are among them. All three are members of the nightshade family, having the capacity to produce solanin—a highly toxic substance. Therefore some people avoid eating them.

Peppers are considered the mildest, captivating cooks and gardeners with their many varieties. Green, red, orange, yellow and purple peppers appear locally, in a range of sizes from the ever popular large bell to tiny fingertip, flavored from sweet to spicy hot. **Jalapeno** is favored for spicing up popular Southern Continent dishes. Our grower claims the **Serrano** is the true pepper for Salsa.

The long, larger sweet **Italian pepper** is ideal for sautes and the sweet bells are delicious diced in salads, in strips on a fresh vegetable platter, or stuffed and baked. Corn niblets combine brightly with sweet peppers, whether fresh in salads or cooked dishes. Basil, oregano, thyme and rosemary complement.

Eggplant or Aubergine is especially popular in Italian, French and Middle Eastern cuisine. In Japan it has been both favored and feared over the centuries by the populace—some claimed blindness from eating too much. Originating in Asia, an early variety now being revived, resembles a large creamy white egg and is more delicate of flavor than the large purple eggplant.

Always cooked, eggplant can be served **peeled, chilled and marinated** for salads or pureed for spread; sliced, lightly salted and pressed to remove bitterness, then **breaded** to saute for parmesan style or **Greek Moussaka**; or cubed to be cooked in ratatouille and vegetable stews. Seasonings include curry, basil, oregano, rosemary and thyme.

Tomatoes, from beefsteak to cherry, have fans favoring one over another. Italian pomodoro, famous in sauce, is liked sliced fresh too. Large tomatoes can be served **broiled, baked or fresh**—herbed or stuffed. The Incas ate only yellow low-acid tomatoes. Explorers brought back the red variety to Europe, where they became popularly cultivated.

Notes

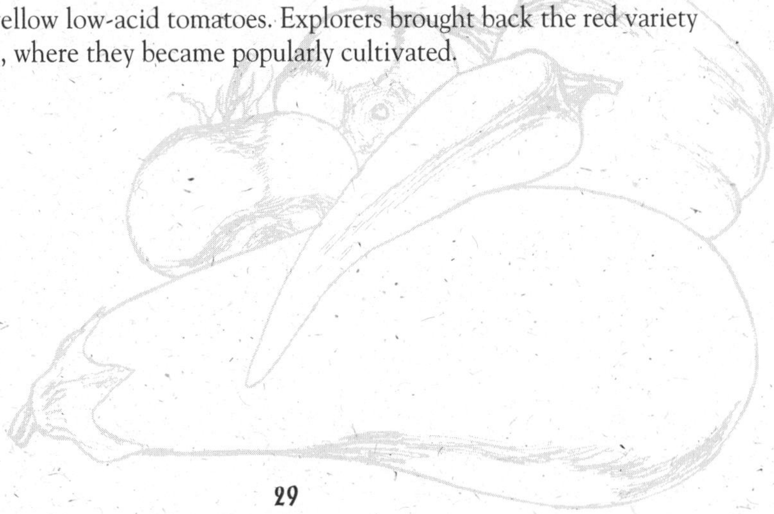

August's 4th Week

Celery

Refreshing, juicy, tall green stalks of celery are a staple of the Summer kitchen. Sliced or minced they add crunch to all kinds of salads, subtle flavor to hot or chilled soups and lighten Summer vegetable stews. Celery sticks can solo in the picnic basket, as an appetizer, and as party fare. Their ease of preparation is welcomed by the cook as well.

Europeans have seen celery as an aphrodisiac and think this is the reason Americans like to chew celery at parties! Whether this or the fact that it can be served with a variety of tasty dips and fillings, celery is a favorite.

Beyond cream cheese and peanut butter, **fillings** can range to the exotic. Consider ground nut-thickened basil pesto; minced Feta cheese, Greek olives and oregano; nut butter, tomatoes, and chives; curried small curd cheese or lentils with pineapple and parsley. For eye-appeal, place 4 or 5 filled celery sticks together—edges slightly overlapping—and slice crosswise into 1/2" scalloped rounds.

Celery also **enhances sauces** such as Remoulade. Lingering in my memory is the delicious one served on a green salad at an elegant plantation restaurant in New Orleans. The closest recipe subtly combines mustard, horseradish, paprika, salt, minced celery, parsley, garlic and green onions marinated in lemon juice and oil with bay leaf. Remove bay leaf before serving.

Italians like to serve celery between courses at a meal to bring agreeableness for the food already eaten as well as **cleanse the palate** and **stimulate the appetite** for the next course. In Japan celery is the base of a month-long cure, and in Europe its **cleansing qualities** are recommended for gout, diabetes and rheumatism. Recently claims have been made for celery as a **nerve tonic**.

The French prefer their celery to be creamy white—as they do asparagus—keeping it soil covered as it grows for a delicate flavor. Sun-drenched green garden celery is popular here in the U.S. While more robust, it is also higher in nutrients.

Green celery leaves and celery seed, strong in flavor, are used as **culinary herbs**. Adding a handful of chopped leaves into the soup pot strengthens its taste and nourishment. The aromatic oil of the seeds stimulates digestion.

CELEBRATE CELERY!

Notes

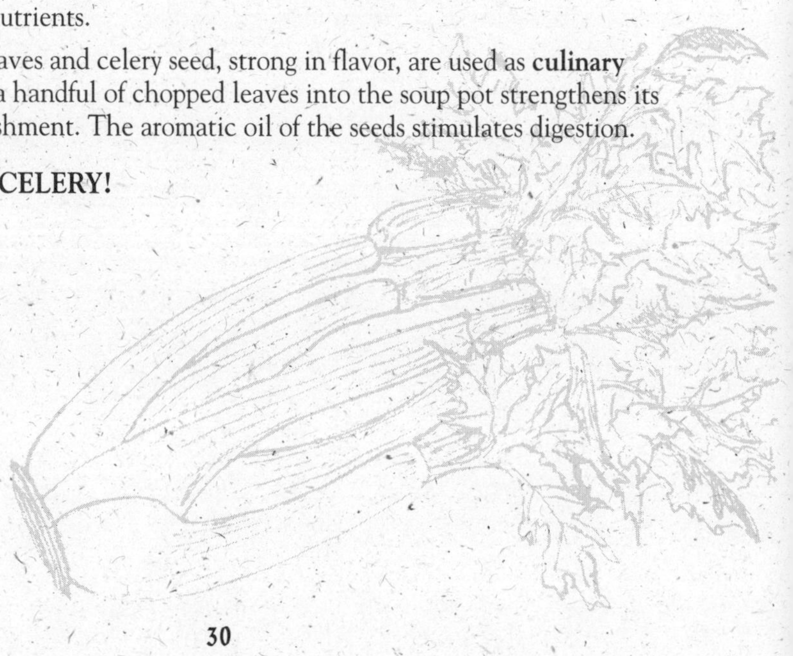

Shell Beans

Summer shell beans—fava, flageolot/French horticultural, and lima included among them—are enjoyed fresh for a few short weeks while young and tender. Most shell beans are grown to full maturity, then dried for pantry storage and year-round availability.

A soft, mealy, almost buttery texture characterizes fresh shell beans. They are considered a delicacy in some cuisines, notably the French and Italian, where special seasonal recipes are a tradition. Often enjoyed as a starchy side dish, they are also rich in protein.

Shell beans are mature seeds of the legume family of nitrogen-fixing plants, whereby up to 40% plant protein is enclosed in their starch cells. This composition is much harder to digest than the protein from animal products. Beans need to be **well cooked** for enjoyment, and are best eaten when soft enough to crush easily between thumb and forefinger.

Fava beans, an Italian favorite, are seeds of a perennial vetch plant to which 5% of Mediterranean males are highly allergic. The rest of the population enjoys the beans cooked in a variety of combinations. One is to cook them, then cool and marinate with artichoke hearts in a lemon juice and oil dressing. A pinch of dried mustard and a few fresh oregano leaves bring a superb flavor. Serve chilled as a side dish or in a tossed green salad.

Aficionados of fresh shell beans are divided between those preferring the small, early ones and those with a penchant for them harvested later and larger. The above recipe is usually prepared with the larger size fava bean. The French on the other hand enjoy their flageolet beans tiny and young, mixed with other vegetables in cassoulets and soups or with herbs as a hot side dish. Savory, marjoram and dill are the favored herbs for flageolets.

All-American **lima beans** likewise have fans who will only eat the thin tender babies while others acclaim the bigger, fat ones as "butter that melts in your mouth". Native Americans planted their beans with corn—the beans bringing nitrogen to the growing corn and the corn stalks serving as poles for the climbing beans. Corn and limas cooked together in succotash was introduced to early Colonists by the Narragansetts and spread continent-wide into regional variations. Dill, nutmeg or paprika are complements.

Notes

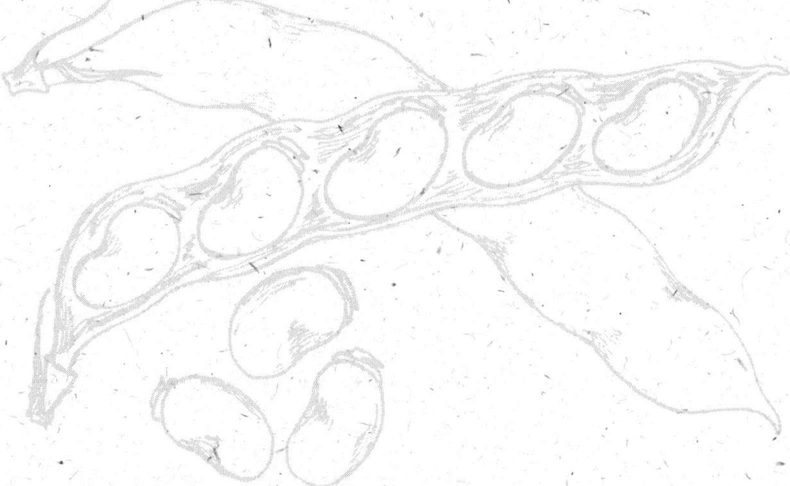

Notes

SEPTEMBER

September's 1st Week

Hardy Greens

Arugula and all the members of the chicory family—endive, escarole, radicchio, witloof (Belgian endive)—follow us from Summer into late Fall with their ability to withstand frost. Then in one form or another, under cold frames and in sand in the basement, some are grown through Winter, bestowing freshness and variety into that Season's fare.

Now in late Summer we mix them with other greens for more robust salads. Their slightly bitter taste comes from a crystalline substance, Taraxacein, flowing up into the leaves from a juice produced in the roots. It strengthens spleen, liver, kidneys and other organs in their functions, particularly in preparing us for the cold weather ahead.

Counter the bitterness of the **chicories** with a light lemon or fruit juice based salad dressing and additions of lettuce, sweeter herbs such as basil, and/or fruit slices such as apple or grapefruit.

Sturdy leaf, deep red and white **radicchio** brightly colors tossed salads and fresh garnishes. Cutting them cross-leaf into ribbons pleases even finicky eaters. Add strips to sandwiches too. The tender inner leaves are best for salad. Reserve the tiniest for serving whole.

- Did you know radicchio can also be **grilled**? I first enjoyed it this way in Pisa, Italy and have tried it since at home. Lightly brush with oil or marinade and sear on a hot griddle. Takes only a minute on each side, pressing them down with a pancake turner. I find this a good use of the heavier outer leaves. Try them over the charcoal, brushed with salad dressing and pressed between a hamburger grate.

Leaves of **escarole** and **endive** can be served fresh in similar ways as radicchio. They can also be steamed or braised and served as a hot vegetable. A popular Italian soup combines escarole cut in strips, and macaroni in a **broth** flavored with onion, thyme, and nutmeg.

Cone shaped **Belgian endive** grow out of the rootstock of previously harvested green heads of leafy endive. Their shape and creamy white color comes from their being grown in a dark, cool environment. They leaf out as soon as exposed to sunlight—hence Belgians housewives carry them from the grocer's in a covered basket. They are cut into crisp 1/2" rings or separated leaf by leaf for serving fresh. They are a delicacy when **braised** or **steamed** whole or quartered lengthwise—a dash of nutmeg for seasoning.

Notes

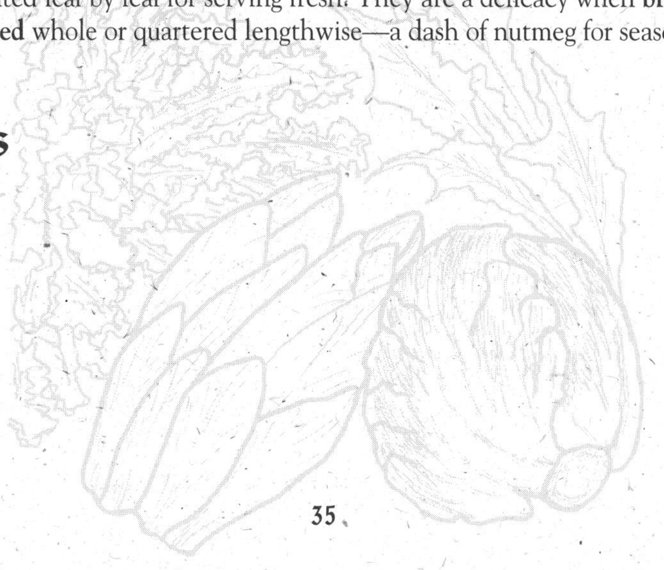

September's 2nd Week

Sweet Fennel

Making a short but sweet appearance from the gardens of adventuresome Northern growers, fennel adds yet another note to our medley of summer vegetables. Related to the carrot and resembling celery, it combines the sweetness of one with the juicy crispness of the other, while being more delicate then either.

In Ancient Greece, fennel was significant in the Eleusinian Mysteries and celebrations centered around Persephone and Demeter—the seasons and plants for food. It was planted in the Temple garden to honor the gods and worshippers crowned their heads with its airy fronds.

The aromatic essential oil characteristic in fennel permeates the whole plant with qualities that **aid digestion and bronchial coughs, sooth nerves, stimulate glandular secretions and help eyesight**. The oil concentrates in the seeds, which are familiar to us as a seasoning and an herbal tea.

Fennel thrives in the warm but not too dry areas of the Mediterranean with a long hot fall—hence its popularity in Italian and French cuisines. The elongated knob of the mature plant forms where the stalks grow from the stem and is delicious **cooked whole**, in quarters or cut into vertical slices.

To **steam or braise** the knob, cut off the green stalks where they separate out, and quarter or slice thickly if large. A dash of nutmeg or a few coriander seeds are enough to complement the delicate flavor of fennel— scallions and lemon juice are also options. Cook until fennel is fork tender and slightly translucent. Add snips of the green fronds near the end of cooking.

A favorite soup in our restaurant was **Fennel Soup Avignon**. We cut up the stalks and any tougher outer parts of the knob, with a little onion and cooked them in vegetable stock with potato cubes or millet, seasoning as above or with a little salt and pepper. It was then pureed, and grated apple was added just before serving.

Fennel Soup Provencale is made similarly, but not pureed, with the addition of flageolot beans. Recently we added pieces of ripe yellow plum and it was equally delicious!

Thin slices of fennel knob or cuts of stalks are delicious fresh. Use in Waldorf salad, mix with pear cubes, or toss with greens. Garnish with its fronds.

Notes

September's 3rd Week

Chokes

Artichokes and Jerusalem artichokes come from quite unrelated plants, each thriving in entirely different climates. The familiar green globe artichoke is the edible immature flower of a thistle-like plant of Mediterranean origins, while the Jerusalem artichoke is the root tuber of a wild sunflower, native to America.

Fortunately for us, both may be available now from local gardens. The globe artichoke season is brief and scant in the North, requiring more tending in cultivation. The sunchoke—as the Jerusalem artichoke is more aptly called—grows wild and wantonly underground, able to be harvested from Fall through Spring, due to its high sugar content.

One similarity in the artichoke and sunchoke is their **favorable qualities for the diabetic diet**. The artichoke contains a natural form of insulin, which is easily digested. The sugar in the sunchoke is inulin, harder to digest, but able to form a diabetic-friendly fructose.

There are many ways to prepare the prolific sunchoke and a number of herbs and spices to complement its qualities. Anise and fennel seeds are good choices, not only for taste but also to **aid in digestion**—soaking **sliced or grated** for an hour in diluted lemon juice is also good. Chives, dill, chervil, parsley, sage, coriander and mace are other choices.

Grated raw sunchoke can be **mixed with apples** and nuts for a salad or for breakfast as a muesli, with the addition of oat flakes. Grated carrots are also tasty in either recipe.

For a **vegetarian burger**, mix oat flakes, minced onions, sunflower seeds, lemon juice, oil, seltzer water and seasoning together with grated sunchoke. Dredge patties in sesame seeds and bake in a lightly oiled pan or grill on top of the stove.

Sunchokes can be **sauteed, steamed, simmered and mashed**—as is, or with other vegetables. Being starch free, they combine nicely with potatoes and grains in various dishes.

The **globe artichoke** is best enjoyed simmered in a non-metallic pot, with water and a little vinegar or lemon juice. Serve hot or cold. We cut off the top third, simmer them stems up and serve with a basil vinaigrette dressing.

Notes

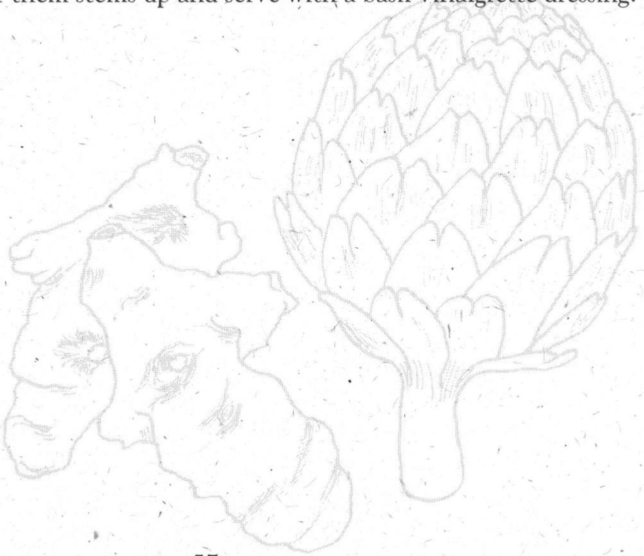

September's 4th Week

Cauliflower

Creamy white cauliflower, with its fleshy flowered head, is closely related to broccoli—but much milder by comparison. Whereas broccoli gathers its color and high nutrient content from exposure to the sun, white cauliflower shuns the sun, wrapping itself in its own thick green leaves or requiring cover from growers. The pale green or purple varieties we see occasionally, lean more towards broccoli.

Cauliflower has similar requirements for preparation as broccoli—blanching before serving fresh, and light cooking when serving hot. Serving blanched and fresh is ideal for arthritis, as its natural sodium content is said to help excrete troublesome acid.

It is delicious **served fresh** with various dips, such as guacamole, hummus, curried or herbed yogurt. Dill and basil complement fresh cauliflower.

Combine separated, **blanched florets** of cauliflower with other vegetables for a refreshing garden medley salad. Corn, red peppers, minced red onion, and olives give a south of the border flair—chopped tomato is an option too. Cucumbers or dill pickles, celery, green beans and snow peas are also tasty additions to cauliflower salads. Serve with a mustard vinaigrette or curried yogurt dressing.

Lightly cooked cauliflower is nice **marinated** in dressing and served chilled—also a good use of left-over florets or stem slices. The stems are very nutritious and can be peeled, blanched and sliced into salads or cut into sticks as snacks for children.

Another treat is to **dip** cauliflower florets in pancake batter and **bake** on an oiled pan in the oven. Nutmeg in the batter heightens the flavor.

To serve the head **whole**, simmer in a little water with fennel or caraway seeds, keeping the cover slightly ajar to allow sulfur to escape. Sprinkle with paprika or a little nutmeg or serve as is—some say dash with a little salt, some prefer none. The leaves may be chopped and cooked with it, as well as minced onion, sweet peppers, corn or other seasonal vegetables. In that case thicken the juices and serve with the vegetables as a sauce.

We like to serve cauliflower with **pea soup** or **topped** with a pureed spinach or leek sauce on a bed of grains.

Notes

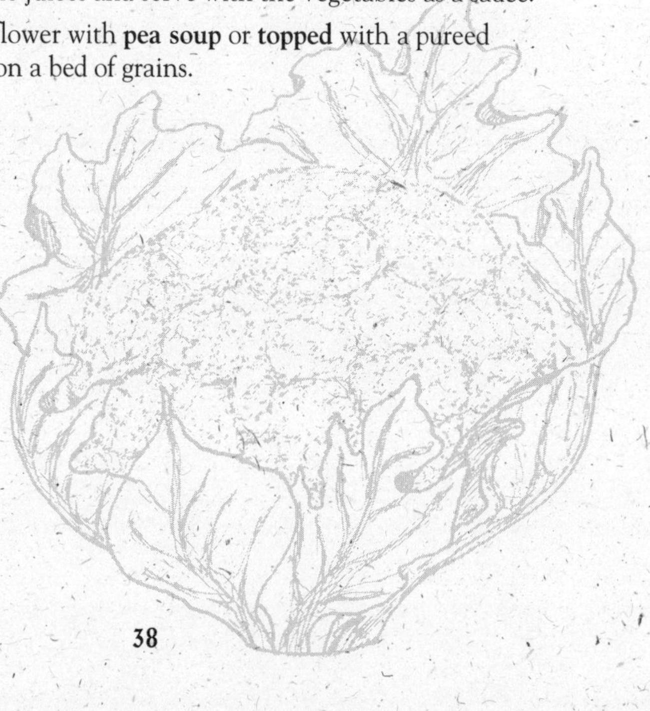

OCTOBER

October's 1st Week

Leeks Take The Lead

Looming large now are the tall green broad leaves of leeks, coming into their own in the Fall garden. Undaunted by the approaching cold, they remain hardy into Winter. Their tender, white, stem-like bulb is very mild and the sturdy thick green leaves, stronger in flavor but with a sweetness unknown in Summer scallions.

Leeks gather soil as they begin to leaf up from their earth-covered stems. Their roots often hold soil and small stones as they arrive at the market. Thus they may require a little more attention in cleaning. Their flavorful goodness, however, far surpasses any effort to prepare them.

If leeks arrive from the garden heavily soiled, **soak** the root end for a short time in a pot of cold water, **swishing** to loosen earth and stones. In this way the rinse water can be poured off outdoors or through a sieve, keeping stones from going down the sink drain.

Leeks usually arrive pre-washed at the market and need only a little more washing just before use. Holding root upwards, **slit vertically** with a knife from about an inch or so above the green—where a little pocket of soil is gathered between leaves and stem—down the center of the green leaf section. Open a bit at bulb top to reveal soil and swish clean in water, being sure to hold root upwards so soil and water run away from the white bulb stem. Wash away any soil remaining on the leaves and drain, root up.

The leaf section may be severed from the white bulb stem and each used separately. Store severed whole leaves or bulbs, covered, in the refrigerator. As with any onion, it is best to use soon after cutting to maintain the mildness of flavor.

Small leeks or the leek bulb may be **lightly sauteed or braised whole**—a delicacy sprinkled with nutmeg or allspice. Serve with polenta or millet.

Combine leeks and barley for a warming **soup or stew**—hearty with carrots and turnip cuts. Sliced leek greens are delicious in soups, sauces and vegetable stews. Season with sage and thyme.

Sliced leeks over chopped spinach or sauerkraut on a whole grain pizza or flat-bread make scrumptuous fare. No wonder leeks take the lead!

Notes

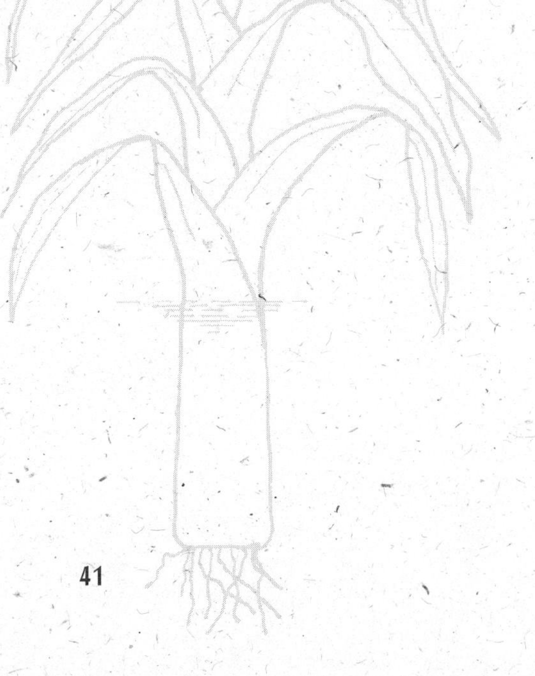

October's 2nd Week

All The Fall Squash

Fall's harvest delights the eye and warms the spirit in its colorful array of orange, yellow, green, blue and white smooth, bumpy, ridged and stripe skinned native American squash crowding farm stands and markets. Visions arise of its pale gold to deep yellow nourishing flesh steaming on our plates for many a meal well into Winter!

Containing ten-fold more vitamin A than its Summer sisters, Winter squash is also rich in silicic acid, carrying light and warmth from the Sun in its sweetness. Match it with maple syrup for true New England goodness. Drizzle it on baked or steamed halves or slices; whip it into mashed squash dishes—especially enticing to children.

We like to **bake** our squash whole and then when almost fork-tender, halve and finish face-up to brown a little. Scooping out the center, we enjoy some of the tasty browned seeds which are rich in zinc.

A saucy mixture of vegetables and herbs **spooned** into the center completes the entree. When lima beans are fresh, they are included, along with chopped onion and carrots. Later in the season, pecans or roasted chestnut pieces replace beans, as do little cubes of tofu.

Sage and thyme complement **Winter squash**—ginger, curry, or allspice too. Add your favorite to a squash soup, redolent with chopped onions or leek. **Simmer** altogether, puree, and stir in some grated fresh squash—unpeeled for color if skin is tender—heat to piping and serve.

In Paris, I enjoyed an excellent **puree** of squash mixed with tiny flakes of grated carrot, garnished with almond slices and served on a vegetable platter with cauliflower, sliced carrots and apples.

Chunks of golden squash are good in a Fall vegetable stew. Add some rosemary for remembrance! **Thicken** pot juices if rich with onion. Other sauces to pour over cooked squash or stew are creamy celeriac with thyme; spaghetti sauce with marjoram; or hazelnut, onion, and parsley with nutmeg.

Squash can also be peeled, cut into **julienne sticks** or slices and steamed, baked on an oiled pan, breaded or French-fried instead of potatoes.

Don't forget **freshly grated squash as salad**—with beets or carrots. Parsley, apples and pears are good contributions to squash salad too.

Notes

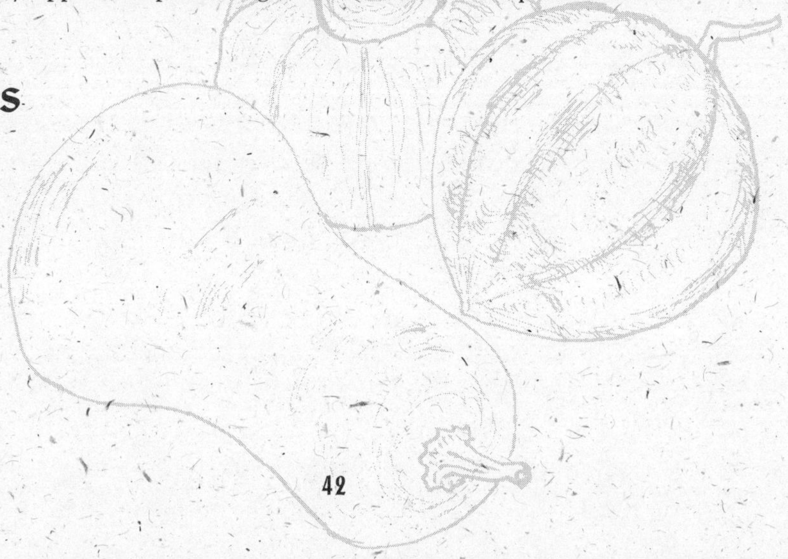

Radishes For Winter

From Western, Middle and Far Eastern cultures come the radishes, to accompany our cold weather table fare, now cultivated locally. Highly valued for healing qualities in ancient cradles of civilization, radishes have their name from the Latin word for root, "radix".

Strong in mustard oil, the European black radish, Oriental daikon and Middle Eastern horseradish are not only able to withstand frosty temperatures, but are at their best from Autumn until Spring. With the warming of the Earth, their vitamin content and crisp texture dissipate, turning them woody and rubbery.

These hardy radishes store well with other root crops, like carrots and beets, and also mix well with them in the kitchen. Their strong flavor imparts a bite that **activates metabolic juices** while perking up recipes and the spirits of partakers. It is said that when one needs stimulation for thinking, it is good to add radish to the menu.

Coarsely grated **black or daikon radish** contribute to a delicious cold-weather salad, tossed with finely grated beets or carrots. Grated apple and chopped parsley can also be added or tossed by themselves with radish. Simply superb sprinkled with lemon juice! No oil please, as it makes the salad heavy and the radish hard to digest.

Radishes are best **prepared just before use**, not ahead, to prevent oxygen from destroying their flavor and good qualities—vitamin C among them. They also have a protein content that is especially complementary to **buckwheat**. When served together, it seems they form a complete source of plant protein having value in human nourishment.

A **healing juice** can be extracted from grated radish. In Europe, honey is mixed with the grated radish, drawing out the juice, which is then strained and served to one suffering from cough of colds or bronchitis. Children are happy to drink every drop. The remaining pulp is enjoyed as a spread for whole grain bread.

In Macrobiotic cooking, daikon is **added to miso soup**—also cooked with other vegetables. Cooking some radish in turnip dishes **assists digestibility**.

Horseradish has intensified radish qualities, and in minute quantities is good in salads—as above. It's snappy with beets and flavorful in creamy dairy or tofu sauces to top Winter vegetables and grains.

Notes

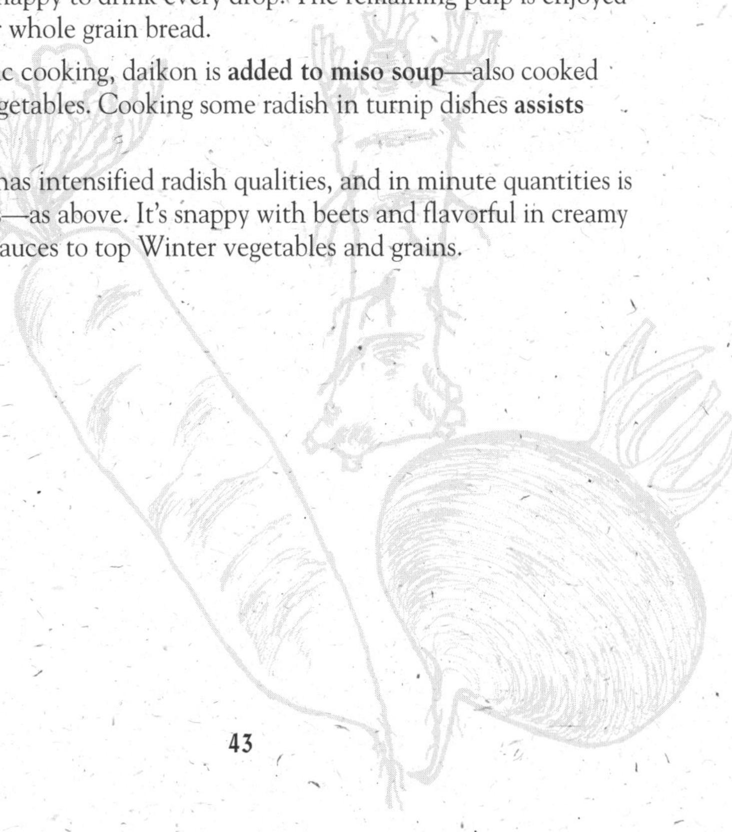

Collard & Mustard Greens

Chinese cabbage and bok choy are actually mustard greens, only distantly related to the cabbage family, while collard greens fall into a classification in between. These leafy greens, more resistant to frost than cabbage, can be harvested late into Fall. Chinese cabbage also stores well for a couple of months in the root cellar.

More lettuce-like in taste and texture, Chinese cabbage—or napa, as one popular variety is known—makes a refreshing crunchy salad. A standard favorite in our restaurant, we cut it on a diagonal across the light green leaf and white stem into thin slaw-like ribbons, then tossed it with a toasted sesame seed vinaigrette dressing.

Napa can also be **lightly cooked**, brightening the pale green of the leaf. Slaw-like napa ribbons are delicious in a Japanese style **miso soup**, or quickly **stir-fried** with fresh ginger and tamari. Marjoram and thyme complement Chinese cabbage.

Cooked millet, cauliflower buds and roasted cashews or sunflower seeds make a nice **filling for napa cabbage rolls**. Simmer shortly and serve as an entree with a light tamari and vegetable broth arrowroot-thickened sauce.

Collard greens are also tasty **stuffed** with a buckwheat or oat filling. Add lightly sauteed grated carrots and minced leek to the filling, seasoning with tarragon or thyme. Wrap in blanched collard leaves, and simmer until deep green and tender (10 mins.) Serve with a mustard sauce.

Collards are strong in flavor, **high in calcium and vitamins A and C**. Beloved in the South, they are served often, cooked with black-eyed peas and in soul-food dishes. They have **contributed healthy bones and teeth** to generations of rural black and white folks, even when they were too poor to have much else. "Cooking them down" cuts vitamins, but the mineral content is still rich.

Bok Choy, with its broad dark green leaves and creamy white crisp stem, is **milder in flavor** than collards, but more full bodied and nutritous than napa cabbage. It can be prepared similarly to both.

We prefer to **toss choy ribbons with vegetables**, like grated carrots or squash and sometimes apple slices for **salad**; or **stir-fry** with julienne carrots, celeriac, onions and fresh ginger for a satisfying supper—served with millet, buckwheat or rice for a hearty meal.

Notes

NOVEMBER

Pumpkin

Linus is right—there is a great pumpkin!

After Jack-O-Lantern and traditional pumpkin pie come dishes from all over the world:

In Afghanistan 1/2" slices of pumpkin are sauteed 'til fork-tender and golden brown on both sides, sweetened (drizzled with honey or maple syrup after turning) and served with yogurt laced with garlic. We like to saute them with onion rings and fresh ginger, then dash with salt.

Whole Pumpkin, with seeds scooped out and the top used as a lid, becomes an edible 'bowl'. It is steamed, then filled with a rice mixture in China; in Japan it is steamed with broth inside and sauteed vegetables added last for a delicious soup; for a warming supper in Sweden, I had it baked, stuffed with cracked grains, spices and raisins .

Pickled Pumpkin, lactic-acid fermented like sauerkraut, is popular in Germany.

Or try:

- **Pumpkin Soup**—curried, or with ginger, or herbs like celery leaves—lace with onions and maybe maple syrup.
- **French Crepes** filled with sauteed pumpkin and leek. Serve with an herbed white or curried hazelnut/filbert sauce.
- **Autumnal Stew** — simmered pumpkin chunks, carrots, turnips and onions —New England style with sage and thyme.
- **Pumpkin Souffle** or **Entree Pumpkin Loaf or Ring**.
- **Coarsley-grate** fresh pumpkin, toss with chopped pear and parsley for a delectable salad: add lemon juice and oil.
- Serving some as an **appetizer** every day for a week as a cure is said to cleanse the body and blood.
- Pumpkin-Fig oatmeal **cookies**; Pumpkin cake and bread;
- Pumpkin **pancakes** and waffles too—so good topped with spicy homemade apple sauce or maple syrup.
- Pumpkin-apple, plum or orange marmelade—with cloves!

VOTE FOR PUMPKIN!

P.S. When the season's pumpkins are all used up, try winter squash in place of pumpkin.

Notes

November's 2nd Week

Brussels Sprouts

Please be sure to use the final 's' in honor of the place where legend says they originated in ancient times. These tiny "rose-cabbages", as they are called in German, are rich in protein, minerals and vitamins—besides being a more delicate tasting kind of cabbage!

Brussels sprouts grow on very tall stalks with large leaves on top. If you receive them on the stalks, they will maintain freshness much longer. If there is enough storage space in your refrigerator, keep them on the stalk until ready to use. Divide the stalks into smaller pieces if space is a problem. Some say the large top-of-the stalk leaves are delicious as well. Use them first in cabbage-type recipes, saving the sprouts for a special occasion.

We like to serve Brussels sprouts for Thanksgiving Day dinner, **steamed** with grated nutmeg and served with roasted chestnut or fresh sunchoke slices. Water chestnut slices or toasted walnuts are also a good complement.

Leftover, they can be pureed and added to lightly sauteed minced onions for a delicious **soup**. Be sure to add fresh herbs or spices, and heat only 'til piping hot. When making a soup from fresh sprouts, either as a **puree** or a **brothy** type, keep a few of the tiniest to float whole in the soup. The larger ones may be cut smaller or chopped.

For an **entree**, serve Brussels sprouts on top of a bed of curried rice. Sprinkle with chopped toasted walnuts or tamari-roasted sunflower seeds—or serve them on millet with a nut-butter or creamy white sauce poured over.

Fresh Brussels sprouts can be used as **salad**. In that case quarter or halve them and marinate them in your favorite dressing—refrigerating for 8 to 12 hours. Nice with apple and celery added just before serving.

Organically grown, there's no need to wash them. As with cabbage, simply peel off the outer spotty leaves and use! Cut a cross on the top for quick cooking. Caraway, dill, parsley or mustard are good seasonings for Brussels Sprouts. Just before serving, sprinkle them with lemon juice or add it to the cooking juices or sauces—enhances the sprouts' delicate flavor.

Notes

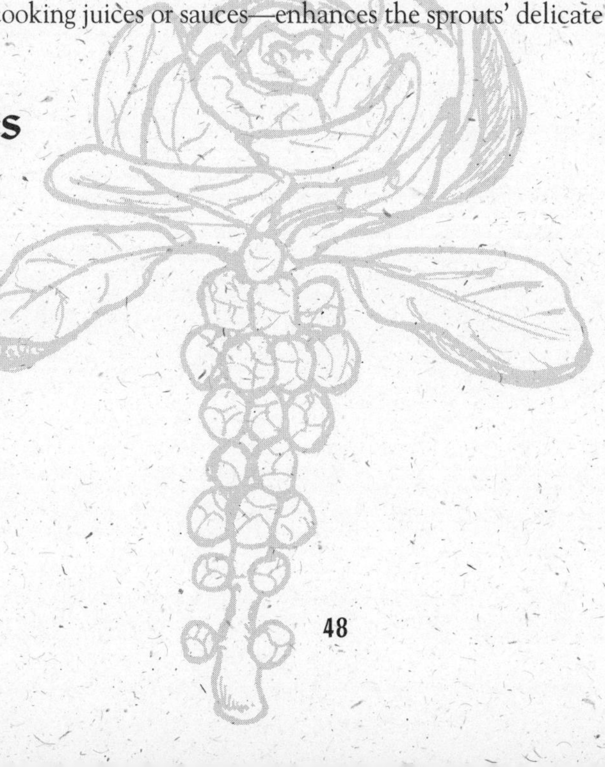

Celeriac

Celeriac—or celery knob—is widely used in the German kitchen, while the wide green stalk variety of celery is a rarity there. Long regarded as one of the healthiest of vegetables, this flavor-packed root finds its way into bean pots, soups, stews—and even into Autumn and Winter salads.

Celeriac is especially good fare for those with rheumatism, diabetes, digestive as well as kidney problems, and is highly recommended in helping to fight colds and alleviate coughs. . . In a good hot soup perhaps?

Lentil soup is always associated with celeriac for me, after watching Lothar put a whole one into a potful he was preparing in his kitchen in Cologne! It made delicious, hearty fare that warmed us through.

It's a tasty addition to root **vegetable soup** as well, with carrot, turnip and onion chunks or cubes. Add thyme in good measure to the pot for well-seasoned stock. **Vegetable stews** are also enhanced with the addition of celeriac.

Consider **cream of celeriac soup**, made with finely grated celeriac, minced onion, and coriander. Of course one can also simmer the vegetables in chunks and puree. Add white or chick pea miso or a splash of cream for richness.

In our restaurant we dredged 1/2" round slices of celeriac in whole-grain flour and sauted in oil to make **vegetarian 'schnitzel' (cutlet)**. Pour over marjoram-spiked spaghetti sauce or a white sauce with nutmeg for a scrumptious entree. To make a similar **casserole**, place rounds of celeriac in oiled baking dish, bake 400°, 5 minutes on each side, dash on thyme and salt, cover with polenta, bake 20 minutes. Top with sauce or parmesan cheese.

Finely grated celeriac complements grated fresh beets or carrots for salad. Add apples—walnuts too for Waldorf style. Splash with lemon juice and oil, or mix with yogurt for dressing.

To clean celeriac, soak a while in water to loosen soil in crevices; scrub well with a brush—little need to peel—and cut away small gnarling roots (use these in vegetable stock). **Clean just before use.** It keeps better soiled.

Notes

November's 4th Week

Thanksgiving

Thanksgiving is a veritable feast—even for vegetarians!

Consider Queen of the Harvest Hubbard Squash, stuffed with wild rice, cracked rye, or bulgar/wheat chestnut stuffing. Of course season traditionally with parsley, sage, rosemary, and thyme—along with minced onion, celery stalks and leaves. Coarsley grated carrot can also be added for color as well as flavor.

We **bake** our **Mother Hubbard** whole—for about an hour if it is large—meanwhile cooking the wild rice or cracked grain; shelling and slicing the previously roasted chestnuts; lightly sauteeing onion, celery (or grated celeriac) and carrot; and tossing stuffing with herbs.

Then we cut a horizontal **slice off the top** of the squash, scoop out the seeds, lightly season the cavity with salt or herbs, and fill with the **stuffing mixture**. Covering with the top slice, we bake this scrumptious stuffed squash for 30 minutes more—or 'til it is fork tender, but still firm. Bring it to the table on a large platter, lift its lid and serve. It's a colorful dish to behold!

Left-overs from this dish can be **stir-fried** with fresh herbs, onion slices, stuffing, and squash cubes—or heated with broth or miso for a delicious, hearty **soup**. The squash itself can be pureed and added to minced onions sauteed in curry spices or with fresh ginger for another soup.

In addition to stuffed squash, we like to serve freshly cooked Brussels sprouts for Thanksgiving, and a tossed **salad** made from thin diagonal slices of crunchy chinese cabbage, our favorite dressing and sprinkled with toasted sesame seeds.

Our feast also includes spicy corn relish we fermented in September, sauerkraut style. Fresh vegetable sticks or carrot curls, olives, and organic fresh cranberry, fig, apple, orange and nut relish complete the condiments.

For **dessert** deep-dish pear crumble with nutmeg or mace, and apple-cranberry crisp or pie—spiced with cardamom, coriander and cloves. We drizzle both with maple syrup.

Cold, gray, or rainy, our Thanksgiving is sun-splashed and warm with gifts from the harvest garden. Blessings!

Notes

DECEMBER

Cabbage—Red & Green

Fall cabbage is the only leafy vegetable sturdy enough to keep long after harvest, enriching our largely root Winter fare. We can be grateful to the Greeks who cultivated cabbage from the leaves of the oil-seed rape plant.

Rich in calcium and vitamins, Cabbage also contains iodine, iron, and sulfur. The latter contributes to the distinct odor that can seem unpleasant. To counter, keep the cook-pot lid slightly ajar allowing sulfur to steam out. Cook quickly and lightly, serving while still colorful and crunchy for pleasant digestibility.

One may want to **simmer** a delicious, warming red cabbage dish a little longer, so its flavor can mingle with the onions, apple, raisins and spices, but not 'til its soggy please! A little cider vinegar or lemon juice helps to retain its deep red color.

Both red and green cabbage make a tasty **kohlslaw**—combined or separately. Fineness of cut is key to the enjoyment of a good slaw. Try adding a little radish, apple—and even kidney beans for extra interest.

Stir-frying is one of the easiest ways to prepare tasty cabbage. Sliced more coarsely than for kohlslaw, it can be stir-fried in combination with other vegetables (e.g. onions or carrots). A selection of spices and herbs imparts flavors that contribute to the creation of distinctly different stir-fried meals. Try poppy seeds with a few dill seeds; curry with cumin; tarragon with fennel seeds; savory with caraway; or ginger with anise seed, to name a few that are tasty with other cabbage dishes as well.

The **etheric oils of seeds** such as caraway bring warmth to the stomach, **helping the metabolic process of digestion**—as does winter radish. With these added and quick, light cooking, cabbage can be enjoyed even by those with a delicate metabolism. It is helpful for diabetes, bronchitis, rheumatism, kidney trouble, and many other health problems today.

What is **New England Boiled Dinner** without cabbage? Cook the carrots and other root vegetables a little before adding **cabbage quarters** to steam on top and stay crunchy. Sage, rosemary and thyme are the herbs for this dish.

LET'S HAVE MORE CABBAGE!

Notes

December's 2nd Week

Turnip/Rutabaga

The Fall storage-turnip, rightly called rutabaga, ranks high as a Winter vegetable. In Europe it is known as "Swede" or Swedish Turnip, from its association with that country, where it has long been popular.

It has fallen into disfavor in Middle Europe, being one of the few foods of abundance after World War II and eaten day after day. Creative recipes are reviving its appeal, especially among vegetarians.

In Sweden it is **mashed** with other vegetables, and beloved by schoolchildren. My mother used to mash carrots, and sometimes potatoes, into mine to my great delight.

I also remember being intrigued with the tawny flavor of some tiny tender cubes turning up in my **vegetable soup**. It wasn't until years later as an adult cook that I realized these were turnip cubes. Is it any wonder that rutabaga's appearance in the Fall harvest sets me to envisioning delicious dishes featuring this mellow golden staple root?

Newly harvested rutabaga (or other turnips) can be coarsely grated to make a **tasty slaw**, along with other grated vegetables—celeriac, carrot, daikon radish—or tossed with chopped parsley and pear or grated apple. The addition of lemon juice and oil are all that are needed to enhance the flavor of this fresh salad/garnish.

Rutabaga is the base for a **one-pot meal of Autumn Roots Julienne**. Cut scrubbed rutabaga into julienne strips and saute in a little oil in a large pot, adding daikon strips, chopped onion and caraway seeds. After sauteing a bit, add julienne carrots, a good measure of dried leaf marjoram, and some water with vinegar or lemon juice. Simmer covered until fork-tender, salt to taste and serve.

- Options include adding julienne potato slices with the carrots; steaming with apple slices on top the last few minutes of cooking—along with strips of tofu or Swiss/raclette cheese; or serving with grated Romano/Parmesan to sprinkle on.
- The same recipe makes a satisfying **stew** by cubing the root vegetables and adding to cooked barley—or a delicious **soup** in the same manner, adding vegetable broth or a blend of miso and water at the end of cooking.

ROOT FOR RUTABAGA!

Notes

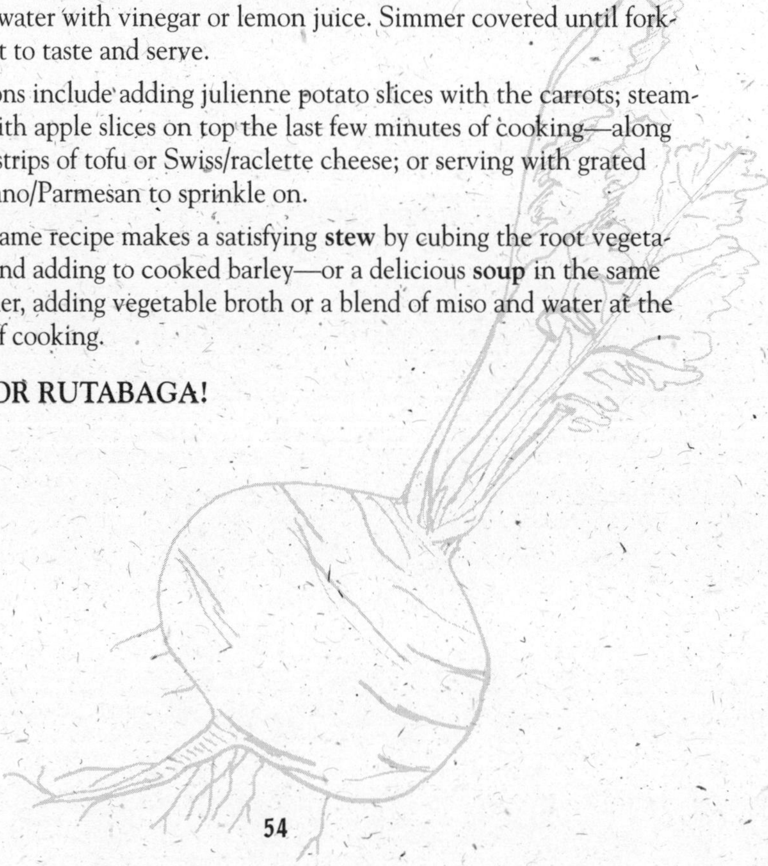

December's 3rd Week

Parsnips A-Plenty

Parsnips are the sweet-meat of the root vegetable family and can be used in numerous recipes, even in desserts fit for a diabetic diet. Not only are parsnips naturally sweet, but they contain inulin—a substance similar to insulin. Cultivated in Europe from a wild strain, they were brought to the new world by the English, who with the French revered them in their cuisines.

High in minerals, parsnips enrich our winter fare, warm us from the inside out, can strengthen a weak stomach, and in olden times were the fare for those with TB or a fever.

Parsnips can be harvested as needed from late Fall into Spring, as long as the ground is not too frozen to pull them out—in which case one waits for a Spring thaw to free them. Wintering over, they become succulently sweet.

Finely grated fresh parsnips make delicious winter salads mixed with carrots, parsley, apple or pear in your choice of combination. Add a little lemon juice and oil to enhance the flavor—chopped walnuts or fennel seeds if you wish.

Simply **saute parsnip slices** with thyme sprinkled over. (Nice served with rosemary-seasoned cooked rye.) Or try parsnips:

- Coarsely grated, made potato **pancake** style
- Cut in chunks with other vegetables for **stew**
- Cooked with curry, onions and pureed for **soup**
- Steamed and **mashed**...with parsley and chives—save the left-overs to make patties, saute both sides crisp; if plain add nutmeg, saute and serve with maple syrup for supper!

Speaking of **sweet treats**,use parsnips:

- In place of, or with carrots in **cake** or **cookie** recipes.
- Instead of pumpkin **in a pie**, add less or no sweetening.
- For a delicious **pudding**. Blend 1C of mashed cooked parsnips and 1C of prunes cooked with cinnamon and thin organic lemon slices. Bring to a boil 1C of water mixed with 1 Tbs arrowroot; add 1 tsp agar-agar flakes (dissolved in 1 Tbs water) and simmer, stirring 5 min. Cool a bit to gel, then fold in parsnip-prune blend. Chill to set. Can be whipped before serving—nice piled high in glass dishes. Garnish with lemon slice or grated lemon rind/zest.
- Try the recipe with apricots and orange, instead of prunes.

Notes

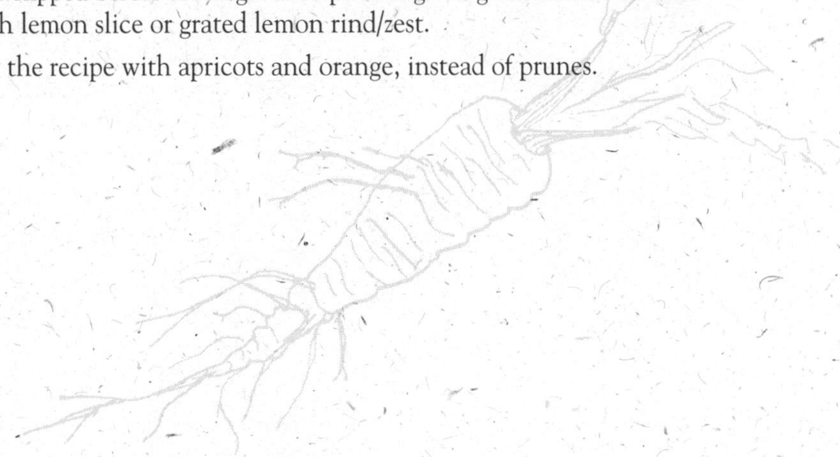

December's 4th week

Festive Fare

Gatherings around the table in Winter's darkness with candlelight and special foods of the Season—heartwarming, flavorsome, colorful—celebrating Light and Hope.

Traditional **potato pancakes** with rosy applesauce; add rosemary leaves for flavor; mix in grated carrots or Jerusalem artichokes for variety. Season the latter with caraway seed for digestibility!

A clove-spicy **red cabbage dish** is a tasty accompaniment; for richness add slices of roasted chestnuts.

Complement red cabbage rolls with green cabbage rolls. Fill **par-boiled** red cabbage leaves with a mixture of **finely grated** beets, lightly **simmered** minced white leek bulb or onion, chopped roasted chestnuts, dried cherries or raisins, allspice and paprika. Sprinkle anise seeds on oiled pan, place cabbage rolls on top and simmer in fruit juice.

Likewise **fill green cabbage** with a mixture of cooked millet, green leek tops, sunflower seeds, minced parsley and tarragon leaves; **simmer** rolls on fennel seeds, with a mixture of lemon juice, water and dry mustard.

Prepare a pot of **tangy black beans** cooked with bay leaf, onion, celeriac, paprika, allspice, chili powder and an organic juice orange—rind grated and flesh cut small—added 30 minutes before serving. **Ladle over:** baked sweet potatoes, cross-slit and pressed open on top.

Include lightly **sauteed or steamed kale or leek** in each layer of your favorite **lasagna** recipe for brighter taste and color. Add thyme in either case!

Serve paprika-topped **polenta** and: kale ribbons stir-fried with allspice; and/or leek tops lightly **sizzled** in oil, dashed with nutmeg, then simmered 'til bright green tender-crisp. In warmer climates, use spinach in place of kale.

A little sea-salt, herb salt or tamari may be added to any of the above dishes to taste. **For warmth**, freshly grated ginger or ground allspice can replace pepper in cold weather

Try whole allspice balls in your pepper mill for Winter!

Notes

Hail To Kale!

Old King Kale is a hearty old Kohl—rich in flavor and nutrients like calcium, iron, vitamins A and C. Kale has reigned in Europe from December through Winter's end due to its heartiness and availability. To many it is considered ready for consumption ONLY after a good frost.

In northern Europe it was washed and hung in a net in windows for decoration—and in the hopes it would freeze through and thus reach its fullness.

A bouquet head of decorative kale appears elegant enough to be carried by a bride or on other festive occasions—later to be **steamed for supper**!

The Scots made it into a **hearty soup**. Thick, cooked with onions and oats and seasoned with thyme, one is warmed to the gills and ready to ward off colds and flu.

Kale was traditionally eaten on Sylvester (New Year's Eve) in Germany to **ward off money problems** in the coming year. Try diagonally sliced kale, lightly **steamed or sauteed** with allspice, and piled high in the center of a ring-mold of barley that has been cooked with bay leaf and rosemary.

Delicious and eye-appealing is **sauteed whole-leaf kale**. Wash in water with added salt (causing any tiny hidden creatures to surface) and stand on stems to drain well. Snip stems off to leaf bottom and saute separated kale leaves quickly on both sides in oil—pressing lightly with spatula—dash with allspice or nutmeg. Let these deep green, crunchy leaves be enjoyed for their full-bodied kale flavor. Use as an emerald leaf bed upon which to serve grains and kidney beans or other vegetables for **warm color contrast**!

Caraway seed is always good with kale, **warming the metabolism** for ease in digestion. Try marjoram leaf as a tasty complement to early kale—with a few fennel seeds for a change. Sprinkle on before lightly steaming or when sauteing.

Kale can also be **served raw**—finely sliced diagonally across the leaf. Mix with other seasonal greens for **kohlslaw;** with red cabbage for festive color; with grated daikon radish—zesty for tastebuds and digestion.

Notes

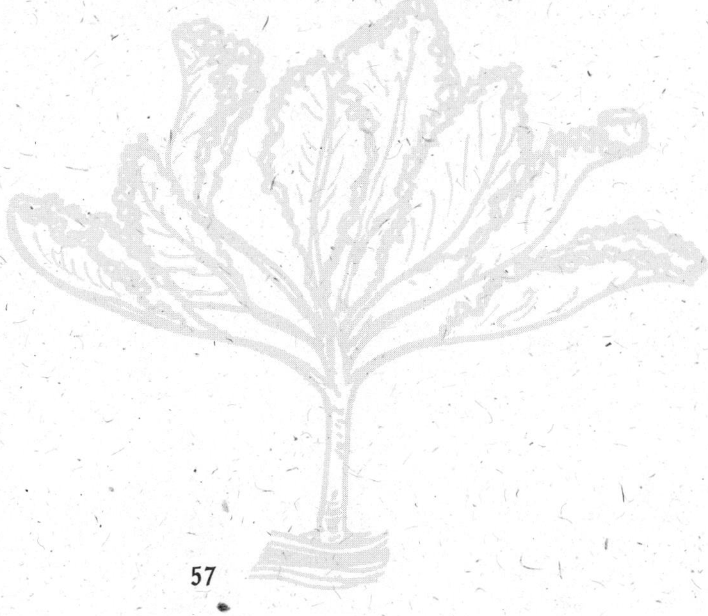

Notes

JANUARY

January's 1st Week

Sweet Potatoes

From the southern reaches of our bio-region, and beyond into Virginia, come sweet potatoes to add color, warmth and lots of vitamin A to our Winter fare. (A small crop can be grown even in northern Vermont.) As we finish the squash stored from Fall, these sweet-tasting tubers arrive on the scene and are marketed well into Spring.

Sweet Potatoes were found by European treasure seekers in South and Central America, along with the white potato. While both seem related by name and have notable starch content, they are from entirely different plant families.

The sweet potato is a true tuber that thrives in sunny climes. Tubers **carry the qualities of grains** for the diets of people in the tropics, especially **chromium**. The dietary importance of this mineral is being recognized in relation to manic depression as well as sickle-cell anemia.

White potatoes are not really tubers, but the swollen stem of this member of the night-shade family of plants, said to grow with the forces of the moon and night. If exposed to sunlight, the white potato turns green with **deadly solanine**, which should be pared away and not eaten.

While the sweet potato was cooked and eaten as a vegetable by the native people of the southern Americas, the white potato was not. Rather it was dried, steamed, then dried and pounded into flour, often to be used as a thickening agent. Europeans began the practice of eating both the white and sweet potato as a vegetable.

Baked sweet potatoes are simply delicious. Besides spicy black beans, prepared Brazilian style, **split and top with lentils** cooked with cuts of organic orange slices and some grated rind for an elegant **entree**.

Other toppings to turn sweet potatoes into a main dish include: curried nut-butter sauce; cinnamon-pecan onion-orange sauce, tamari seasoned and thickened with arrowroot; clove-spiked dried fruit and nut sauce—be sure to include apricots or peaches along with thin organic lemon slices or juice for tang.

Simmer or steam in their jackets on top of the stove too—serve as above or peel and mash. Save left-overs for soup.

Sweet-sour best compliments sweet potatoes!

Notes

January's 3rd Week

Onions

The noble onion—a juicy, aromatic, and flavorful bulb—is an edible gift to humanity from the lily family. In Winter we can be grateful for the enhancing taste it lends to many a dish, sauce or soup. Revered throughout the Ages as healer and health-giver, it still plays a major role in cuisines worldwide today.

The healing properties of the onion have long been used in treating colds—from wrapping slices in a hot cloth and applying it externally for sore throat, to making a syrup of grated onion and honey to drink in hot milk or cider against coughing. Today we are more apt to think of hot soup when treating colds; and that usually implies brothy soups with onions as a base.

Onion soup has become a standard favorite in Western cultures and is seen on most restaurant menus. Here, as in some other recipes, the onion stands on its own as a vegetable. Cook lots of chopped onions in a vegetable or other stock, season with allspice, cloves, thyme or garlic.

Besides serving **creamed** cooked onions with paprika as a dish, consider **baking whole parboiled** onions sprinkled with paprika or a clove in each, served with breadcrumbs—or **filling whole onions** with wild rice, pilaf, or traditional bread stuffing. To do so, peel, cut the bottom flat, spoon out the centers with a teaspoon and fill. Bake or simmer covered for 30 minutes or until appearing a bit translucent.

Thyme, bay leaf, parsley, anise seed and curry are also complementary seasonings for onion dishes.

Sprinkle thyme over chopped onions spread on thin whole-grain bread dough, top with grated Swiss cheese or sesame seeds and bake in a hot oven for **Alsace onion tart**. For **German-style onion kuchen**, cover caraway seed dotted biscuit dough with lightly sauteed chopped onions and butter, cheese, nuts or sesame seeds and bake.

To bring out the best in onions, choose a size that can be used at once as their sulfur content develops a bitterness when exposed to air; freshly peel, slice and cook or serve immediately. NEVER SLICE AHEAD!

How sweet they are!

Notes

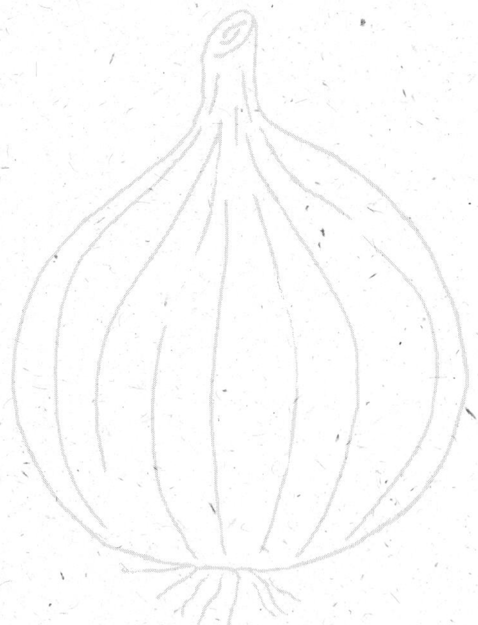

January's 4th Week

Parsley

The green that follows us through the year, parsley grows in garden row, in pots on windowsill, under cold frame and in the greenhouse. The curly type is more hardy—the flat leaf given to warmer climes like Italy.

Thriving since Antiquity, parsley is the most popular of all herbaceous plants. Rich in potassium, it aids digestion; in plant protein, it excels; containing high concentrations of vitamins and minerals, it promotes blood circulation, as well as strengthens the kidneys and the nervous system.

Parsley can be used as an herb to complement almost any dish, as a colorful garnish at the table, and as a vegetable in its own right. In Winter it brings a touch of green to brighten seasonal salads and slaw.

Toss chopped parsley with ribbons of diagonally-sliced Nappa cabbage for a refreshing salad. It is said that cracked-grain **Tabouli** is basically a parsley salad, so be sure to include lots of minced parsley when next you make it! We like our Hummus mixed with parsley too.

For a tasty **Winter salad** or garnish, toss finely minced parsley with equal amounts of fresh or dried shredded coconut and finely grated carrots. Splash with lemon juice and serve—for added flavor, dash with ground nutmeg, coriander or allspice.

Make a **Winter parsley pesto** and use it as sauce—over risotto—as a dip, spread on bread, or on pizza before covering with other toppings. Walnuts in the recipe make it extra good.

Of course add **minced** parsley when cooking a pot of beans, especially with chickpeas and lentils—add some fresh just before serving as well.

Garnish Winter root vegetable stews and soups with minced parsley. There is hardly a soup that couldn't be enhanced with a measure of minced parsley!

If you have lots of parsley, make **parsley soup**. Chop stem and leaf; saute lightly; season with allspice. Add vegetable broth or stock; simmer until piping hot. For heartiness add cooked millet or rice.

Notes

FEBRUARY

Beans

Come into the kitchen on a cold snowy day to a warm pot of beans bubbling on stove-top or in the oven. Heartily cooked with root vegetables for flavor and digestibility, we need add only a grain complement and winter salad for pleasing fare. Every Saturday in cold weather, my grandmother baked beans for supper, along with bread for the week!

Beans were already a tradition as one of the Three Sisters of Life amongst Native Americans when Europeans arrived, and soon were an essential part of the settlers diet. Easy to store, dried beans travelled with families continent-wide and were adapted into satisfying regional recipes. They were valued as a filling staple to be served with corn bread, brown bread, cooked dried corn or rice.

Today we learn the protein content of dried beans **combines well** with that of whole grains, and can form the base of a nutritious vegetarian meal. Much higher in nitrogen-rich protein than grains, a healthy portion of beans is 1/4 to 1/3 that of grains. Too much protein puts stress on liver and kidneys.

For **larger servings** of bean dishes, add lots of carrots, celeriac, and daikon or black radish to the pot—along with flavorful onion, of course! Include a small piece of Kombu/Atlantic Kelp from the New England coast when cooking beans for added nourishment and to aid digestion.

Savory—called bean or pepper-herb in Europe—is good with beans. It brings **warmth to the metabolism**, necessary for breaking down the nitrogen qualities of dried beans. Allspice, chili powder, mustard or curry to taste bring more helpful fire. Cook fresh ginger in a pot of dried pears and lima beans—lace with maple syrup!

It is best to **wash and soak** all dried beans in water to cover over night, then drain and add fresh spring water to cook. For larger, harder beans—like chickpea or kidney—soak, drain, then rinse morning and night for a day or two, as for sprouting. Cook beans slowly in spring water or vegetable broth and a little cider vinegar to help soften. Salt toughens, so add at end of cooking.

My mother **broiled** left-over beans on top of wholegrain bread, topped with onion slices or fruit and maple syrup!

Notes

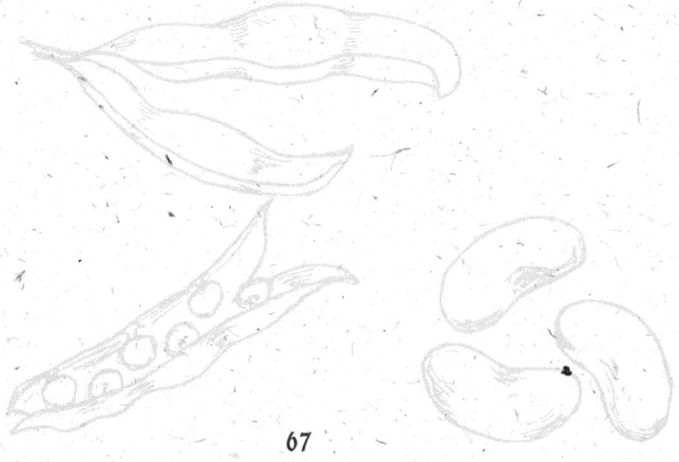

February's 2nd Week

Heart Beets For You

Make Valentine's Day heartwarming with a dish of Red Beet Hearts. Notch out the stem end of whole beets in a "V" shape and then slice vertically from stem to root. Voila! Heart-shaped slices. Season with tarragon leaves and steam or simmer them until tender-crisp. Blend one tablespoon of arrowroot powder to one cup of tart fruit juice (or lemon juice and water) and pour over the hot beets, simmering until the heart slices appear glazed.

A sweet-sour flavor is very complementary to beets. Red sour cherries, raisins, or orange cuts can be added in the cooking for further appeal. Horseradish, freshly grated ginger, mustard or allspice bring good flavor as well.

Long considered important in blood-building, red beets are **rich in minerals**—potassium, calcium, magnesium and iron—to name a few. Strengthening in times of colds and flu, red beets pressed into juice are said to aid in fever.

What is more warming on a Winter's day than a **Red Beet Borscht**. For authenticity add lactic-acid fermented beets or sauerkraut just before serving! Ladle over rice or boiled potato and top with yogurt or tofu blended with horseradish. It's also good with wholegrain rye bread.

If you're cooking with one of the yellow or white strains of beets, try an onion, orange. hazelnut sauce—elegant!

For a **colorful tasty dish**, dice and cook red beets. Combine green pickle relish with yogurt, a white or tofu sauce with optional horseradish and fold into the hot beets and serve.

Or chill this bright pink dish and serve as a **salad**.

Make a red beet **aspic** from red beet/vegetable broth, with grated beets and celeriac added as it sets. A red fruit juice gel is also nice with grated beets and apple—and raisins too!

Finely grated beets and fresh ginger tossed with coarsely grated apple and lemon juice is a really refreshing salad. Similarly combine beets, Winter radish, and parsley with allspice or anise seed.

Finely grated beets are delicious in **breakfast "muesli"**, especially combined with dried fruit!

Notes

February's 3rd Week

Salsify

Known as Black Root in German, salsify or oyster plant is little known in most American kitchens, but is a storage root of a delicacy that deserves wider cultivation here. It brought heightened creativity to us in preparing Winter menus in our restaurant in Cologne. If it is not available to you this year, perhaps sharing some of its uses will entice you or your local grower to plant some for the coming season.

At first cultivated in the 16th century by the Swiss as a medicine against snake-bite, it soon became recognized for its healing properties in cases of epilepsy, heart trouble and weak eyes. A boiled tea of unpeeled salsify slices is given for the kidneys, as well as for rheumatism.

It took the French chefs of 17th Century Haute Cuisine to discover its delicacy as a vegetable. Like other root vegetables, salsify contains minerals, vitamins and trace elements.

To prepare these thin, dark roots for cooking, wash and scrub with a stiff brush. In most cases they are peeled and placed in vinegar water to maintain their whiteness until cooked. They can also be **steamed** with their skins on which allows for easy removal, as the skins become a bit sticky when salsify is peeled raw.

A favorite recipe in our restaurant was **Salsify crepes**, which were served for Brunch or as a dinner entree. We steamed the roots, peeled them and folded them into French Crepes—with yogurt—for Brunch. Nice for dinner with a lemon herb white sauce or light cheese sauce poured over. (A tofu-hollandaise would be perfect, as salsify carries a reminiscence of asparagus.)

Nutmeg, allspice, mustard, tarragon or thyme can be lightly used to enhance the delicate flavor of salsify.

We also added steamed and peeled salsify—whole or in chunks—to **vegetable stews**, raising them from mundane to extraordinary fare, lifting the cook's spirit too!

Peel and grate fresh salsify with apples; add parsley, lemon juice, and chopped nuts for a scrumptious **salad**.

Notes

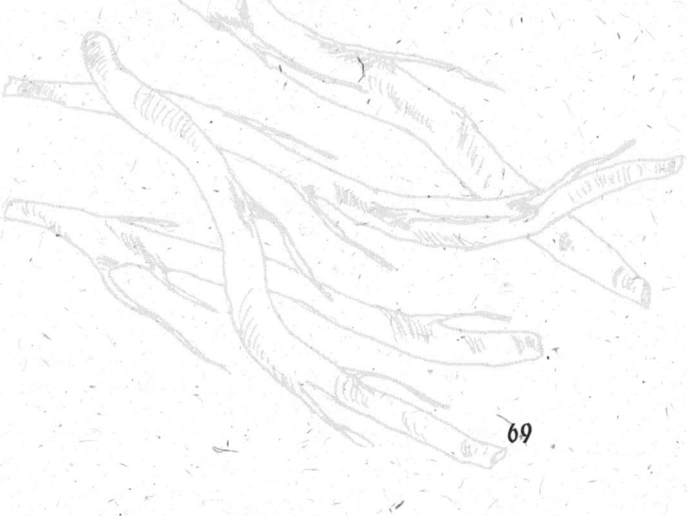

Sauerkraut

Lactic-acid fermented vegetables, of which sauerkraut is probably the best known, rank high as nutritionally enhanced food and are especially good Winter fare. The slightly sour flavor that lactic-acid imparts to cabbage and other vegetables in the process of fermentation can bring us out of the doldrums when appearing on our plates.

Considered "medicine of the kitchen" by Annelies Schoeneck in her long-time work fermenting a variety of vegetables in Sweden, sauerkraut was known to preserve the health of Captain Cook's crew in long sea voyages. It provides acetylcholine for nerves, enzymes for digestion, and vitamins—including B-12 that can only develop in the presence of lactic acid—all strengthening for intestinal flora and immunity.

Most advantageous to use is **fresh, raw sauerkraut** from a known regional source, that is sold refrigerated. When using some from a jar, always press the remainder under the juices, as **oxygen destroys its value**, and keep in the refrigerator. Once opened, use the rest soon.

A Smorgasbord of recipes awaits the adventuresome:

Try a warming **sauerkraut-oat casserole**. Cook whole oat groats, seasoning with thyme or oregano. Layer with hot cooked carrots and top with fresh sauerkraut. Heat in oven only until hot—**sauerkraut loses vital nutrients in cooking!** Cooked beans, tofu cubes or grated cheese can be added to the layers for protein.

Add sauerkraut to **pizza** when it is almost done; top with cheese, crumbled tofu, chopped nuts, or sesame seeds; bake only 'til piping hot and serve immediately.

Top a **vegetable stew** with sauerkraut near the end of cooking for a dish to spark you up.

Add sauerkraut to **tabouli cracked wheat salad**. Make it from scratch with steel-cut oats for a change!

Toss fresh sauerkraut with grated carrots, beets, or celeriac—for a luscious salad; sprinkle with lemon juice and oil. Can add minced parsley, grated apple, Winter radish too!

Notes

MARCH

A Week's Worth Of Roots

Imagine creating tasty appetizing dishes for 7 days from the last varieties of harvest roots. Slim-pickins, it is not! Last year we persevered and were delighted. Here's how:

- **Lentil stew** with onion, celeriac, carrots and winter radish. Seasoning: bay leaf, thyme and savory or cinnamon curry.
- **Carrots** simmered with ginger; served with **millet** cooked with coriander; **nut-butter sauce topping** made with onion, celeriac, lemon juice or cider vinegar, and allspice.
- **Diced beets** cooked with onion, tarragon, anise seeds and cider vinegar or tart fruit juice, arrowroot thickened to glaze; **nutmeg seasoned buckwheat** topped with a creamy mustard white sauce made from milk or tofu.
- **Fill cabbage leaves** with left-over buckwheat mixed with sunflower seeds, lightly sauteed minced onion, grated celeriac and fennel seeds. **Roll up**, sprinkle tarragon or savory on top in pot and simmer. **Glaze** with a mixture of lemon juice, mustard and arrowroot added to pot juices at end.
- **Celeriac or rutabaga cutlet** from 1/2" round slices that are first oiled, then coated with fine bread crumbs or whole grain flour mixed with marjoram and baked 'til crispy outside and tender inside—try **parmesan style** or with **dashes of herb salt or lemon juice**. Nice with rice or served on hearty rye bread.
- **Chunky vegetable stew** from choice of available roots—celeriac, onion, carrots, parsnips, rutabaga—simmered with rosemary and thyme. Add cabbage quarters to steam on top til crunchy tender or sauerkraut to heat through. Complement with miso, tofu chunks, beans or swiss-style cheese. Apple chunks can be added too.
- **Root veggie burgers** on whole grain bread or served elegantly with Native American wild rice and salad. More about veggie burgers next week.

Don't forget to serve **Winter salads** or **garnishes** with the above menus. Sauerkraut tossed with grated roots; red or green/white cabbage slaw; parsley, coconut and grated roots or grated root Waldorf salad—to name a few.

Notes

Burgers, Pies & Pate

It's time to begin using up the storage roots and find appetizing ways to serve them. Reserving some special recipes that become favorites as Winter transitions to Spring help to perk up spirits and weather us through.

Take the makings of a root vegetable stew; cut into cubes or slices and encase them in your favorite pie crust; sprinkle complementary herbs over the vegetables; bake until golden crusted and bubbling with flavor! The aroma and taste will be tantalizing. Parsnip, thyme & onion pie?

The ever popular **burger** can be made in a variety of ways using up the roots:

- Make **veggie burgers** with 2C grated storage roots—could be basically beets or carrots—and 1/4C minced onions, tossed together with herbs or spices and 1Tbs oil. Add a blend of 1C wholegrain flour or fine oat flakes, 1Tbs arrowroot, and 1tsp salt; mix well; form into patties and bake on oiled pan in hot oven. Sunflower or sesame seeds can be pressed on before baking or cheese melted on top at the end. Finely chopped nuts tossed in earlier are also an option.
- Left-over **cooked grains, lentils or chopped nuts** can also form the basis for veggie burgers.
- For **tofu veggie burgers**, lightly saute grated carrots, celeriac and minced onion with fresh ginger or preferred seasonings. Fold into 1 lb mashed tofu mixed with 1/4C oat flour or fine flakes, a little arrowroot, salt or tamari, and minced parsley. Place scoops on oiled pan sprinkled with sesame seeds. Put more sesame seeds on top, flatten and bake in hot oven until golden brown.
- Try the above recipe **using ricotta** or **small-curd cottage cheese** in place of tofu. Add Italian or French herbs.

All of the above can also be make into a **veggie loaf** by placing in an oiled loaf pan and baking in a moderate oven. Consider serving with a sauce to pour over.

Vegetable pates can be made in a variety of ways. As a **baked pate**, use ground sunflower seeds or nuts (not nut butter) as a base, adding minced onion, finely grated or pureed root vegetables, seasonings, flour or arrowroot to thicken, hot water to moisten and some oil. Bake in oiled pan. For **lighter pate**, simmer veggies; season; blend with nuts/ seeds; chill and **spread**—on whole grain bread or crackers.

Notes

March's 3rd Week

Hints Of Spring

Seed-time is coming; the Vernal Equinox approaches; the sun lingers longer in the day. Hints of Spring can appear on our tables with seeds in our fare.

Poppy seeds, for instance, are a nice addition to recipes. Popular in Rumania and Russia, they are sprinkled onto **noodles dishes** and enjoyed with cabbage. Add them to **stir-fried cabbage**—with tarragon for subtle flavor.

Try the same to flavor **vegetable stews or pies.**

- If not in the pie, add poppy seeds to the crust.
- In deference to Rumania, we **add them to cornmeal dishes**. Nice with polenta and in cornmeal muffins or bread, poppy seeds baked in corn sticks add to crispness.
- **Crushed poppy seeds** can be a tasty addition to white sauces to pour over simmered root vegetables. Added dry mustard spikes the sauce a bit, while ground coriander can be a subtle complement.
- Also tasty in all kinds of **dumplings**—from those that cook in soups to the ones that rise to lightness on top of stews or pot-pies.
- Add crushed poppy seeds to **salad dressings**: mustard vinaigrette, yogurt, fruit-juice based; delicious on cabbage or other vegetable slaws.
- **Pocket poppy, sunflower or toasted sesame seeds** with grated roots—such as carrots, celeriac and onions—or shredded cabbage and parsley in **Cornish pasties** or **Polish perogies**. . . or add them to similar fillings in **blintzes** and **crepes.**

Hints of **Spring color show** in the seed forms of corn and peas. **Cornmeal,** ground from dried corn kernels, some of which grow new corn when planted, brings the yellow of new tendrils to our tables. Added to the broth of onion, celeriac or cabbage soup, it brings a pleasing creamy texture as well as a delicate tone. A dash of nutmeg complements.

A **cornmeal batter** can also be poured over slices of onion or celeriac in an oiled pan and **baked** for an **entree**. Top with seeds, nuts or cheese sauce.

Spring-green split pea soup brings a taste of things to come from the early garden. Seasoned with chervil or a light curry of ground coriander and cardamom, it can match the Season while warming against March bluster. For a good use of roots, besides onion, add carrot and/or parsnip slices later to the cooking soup. Top with parsley.

Notes

Sour & Lighter

With the beginning of Spring our thoughts turn to lean and clean. In addition to household and pantry, annual nutritional cleansing has long been the order of the Season in cultures worldwide. Essential to health, Spring Fast practices help in lightening oneself to meet Summer and its warmth.

Lighter meals and sour tastes replace the sweeter, heavier foods of Winter, lifting our spirits. In finishing up the stores of root vegetables from last year's harvest, herbs are changed from the strong and warming to those more subtle and sour.

- Use **dill seeds** in cabbage dishes and stews, as the days warm, in place of caraway—which is still nice when the wind blows cold.
- **Ginger** in place of heavier spices aids the liver in its Spring cleansing role. Enjoy it in stir-fry and soups.
- Grated **horseradish** is also good for the metabolic system in Spring. Add it to red beet dishes and simmered root vegetables, as well as grated beet or carrot salads.
- **Chervil** is a traditional herb for Spring in Middle Europe. Known for its rejuvenating qualities, it is especially good in cooking carrots or peas, & in vegetable soups and broths. Use it in place of thyme now.
- **Parsley**, of course, has its importance in cleansing with its high potassium content. Use it lavishly!
- **Sauerkraut** also has its place in the Spring kitchen. Feature its light sour taste in fresh salads or garnish. Lactic-acid fermented carrots are refreshing now too.
- **Prunes for Spring** lend surprising elegance to simple fare. Quarter them and add to a brothy lentil vegetable soup, along with thin slices of lemon. Be careful not to cook too long—biting into a fruity nugget is the delight! For the finishing touch, complement with minced ginger and parsley.

Prepare a pot of **parsnips and prunes** simmered with lightly sauteed onions, seasoned with coriander and strewn with minced parsley on a cold Spring day. Toss in some toasted almonds and serve on a bed of cooked whole rye berries flavored with leaf tarragon. Nice with a grated carrot or beet and cabbage slaw.

Notes

APRIL

The Bitter Herbs

Taking our cue from Mother Nature, the bitter herbs—sour, stronger flavored—are featured in the special dishes of Spring. Cultivated or gathered wild, these green harbingers of Spring have been recognized from ancient times as health-giving gifts. The bitter herbs of Spring are vital for our cleansing and revitalization to transition from Winter to warm weather. First noticeable are the thin green spikes of tiny wild onions pushing up everywhere and the appearance of water cress along meadow rivulets and Spring streams.

Gratefully we sprinkle fresh snips of baby onion chives as broadly as they grow—on salads, soups, sauces, crepes, and sandwiches—mixing them into spreads and dips. Even children can enjoy their mild flavor! In Northern Germany chives are considered the most important kitchen herb and are mixed into pancake batter for a tasty Spring Supper.

Water cress, whether the fine variety gathered wild or the thick-stemmed larger leaf type cultivated for market, is **high in Vitamin C** and considered to have anti-biotic as well as blood purifying properties. A strong herb, water cress is **best mixed with other greens or vegetables** for salads. A few green sprigs make a nice garnish for any dish. Save the thicker main stems to chop and add to soups. Swish-wash water cress in cold deep water to clean; spin or drain well; keep crisp in a damp towel in refrigerator produce drawer.

Sorrel, known as sour grass to some, has long been a favorite in the French kitchen for Spring, along with chervil. These two herbs can be served separately or together in their **fresh green state**. Chopped, they are a nice addition to Spring soups or sauces. Sorrel **aids digestion**, stimulates kidneys and nervous system, as well as the appetite. Toss a few minced leaves into salads—or simmer whole and serve bright green.

Early **dandelion greens**, foraged in the wild or of the cultivated market variety, are also noteworthy for Spring cuisine. Gathering goodness from the Sun to bestow on man, these green leaves bring valuable bitters and other nutrients to strengthen liver and gall bladder, as well aid in arthritis. A European Spring cure includes a little chopped fresh daily in salads. It's also tasty **quickly steamed** or **lightly sauteed** in a little oil.

Notes

April's 2nd Week

Kale's Back

As the snow recedes in the northern part of the country, hearty kale that has wintered-over from last season's planting appears bright and green as it leafs out for Spring picking. Strong in flavor that borders on the bitter, and packed with vitamins and iron, kale can fortify us through the vulnerability of our body's seasonal transition from cold (and colds) to warmth.

Kale is especially welcome in fresh green Spring salads. Swish-wash in a cold water bath (hardly an insect on it this time of year) and drain or spin. Finely cut slaw-style on a slight diagonal across the leaf, from top to bottom where the stem thickens. Save the stem portion for soups.

It's nice served on its own tossed with a light lemon juice and oil dressing—with a few dill seeds added if you wish. Leaf tarragon, dried from last season, can be a subtle complement in the dressing. **Tossing Kale slaw** with other grated root vegetables makes a refreshing salad as well, perhaps with Winter radish.

PARSNIPS TOO return to our kitchens—newly dug and sweet from their wintering-over in the now thawing ground. In the midst of the muddy season, **the Earth still provides us with vital and tasty foods** that perk up our table fare as well as our spirits.

Steam, lightly simmer, or stir-fry slices of parsnips with ribbons of kale leaf and/or rings of kale stem for a dish combining the bitter with the sweet. For more color, add carrot slices. Season with coriander, which complements them all; and strew with chive snips just before serving.

Toss **grated fresh parsnips** with chopped parsley and chives for salad. Grated horseradish can also be a snappy addition—cleansing for Spring as well. Snips of soaked, uncooked prunes in parsnip salad can spark appetites too. Dress with lemon juice and oil—maybe with added poppy or sesame seeds—or dress with yogurt.

Parsnips can also form the base for **pate**, as presented in March. Try them as a layer in a loaf pate—as colorful and tasty as the ones I enjoyed in London—green, orange and white on a thin pie crust. Separately blend simmered kale, carrots, and parsnips; season and jell each (with agar-agar); add a layer as the one below sets to a firm jelled state.

Notes

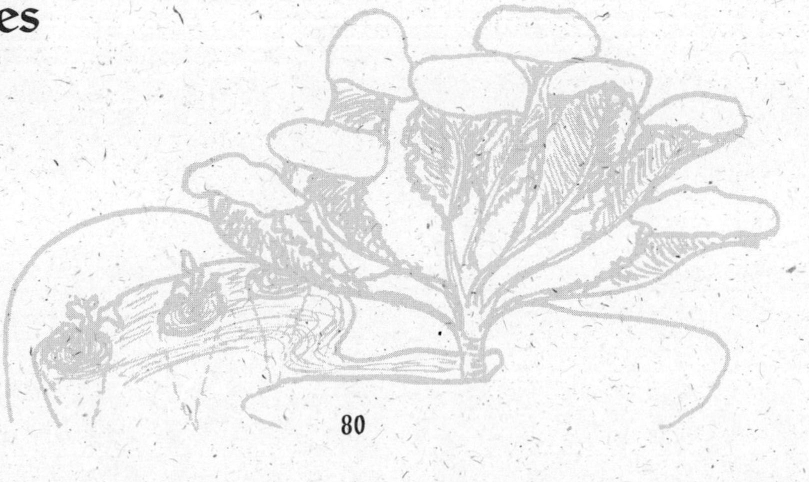

April's 3rd Week

Greens Under Glass

From under the glass of cold frames, come heartier greens that Winter-over in a dormant state until the warmer rays of March's sun bring them to life again. In a few short weeks they provide us with fresh greens for April salads.

Small deep green leaves of Mache or Corn Salad—probably the heartiest of the lot—make their appearance first. In Germany they are called "Feldsalat" (Field Salad). We received them from our growers as soon as snow no longer covered them so they could be harvested. Resembling a miniature spinach plant, Mache has a few leaves growing out of a small root stem. It usually comes to market with the leaves still joined to the root stem. Unlike spinach, Mache does not contain oxalic acid and can be enjoyed by all.

To prepare Mache for a tasty **Spring Salad**, swish wash them in deep cold water. Since the stem root is often tender and edible, it is not necessary to pluck off the leaves. They may require a second or third swish wash in clean water if sand or soil is in the stem joint. Thereafter spin or drain well. Delicious tossed with a lemon juice and oil dressing and sprinkled with toasted sesame seeds, Mache deserves to solo as salad.

We find our **salad spinner** one of the best investments in kitchen equipment—not only is it a time-saver, but a salad saver as well. Extra greens that have been washed and well spun, can be kept crisp and ready for use a day or two later. **Wrap** in a clean damp dish towel and place in the refrigerator vegetable drawer.

I've made different sized salad bags for this purpose by folding a dish towel in half and sewing a seam up two sides, leaving the top open to fill and fold over to maintain freshness. For larger leaves or amounts of greens, **sew** two dish towels together seaming the two narrower ends and the longer one together, keeping one long opening for ease of filling and finding the different greens.

Washed and spun parsley, and other leafy herbs **keep well** with this method as well—either together with salad greens or kept separately in a smaller bag. Launder bags after a few uses to keep clean and fresh. Talk with your grower or grocer to find out what kind of local greens under glass they could supply for Spring.

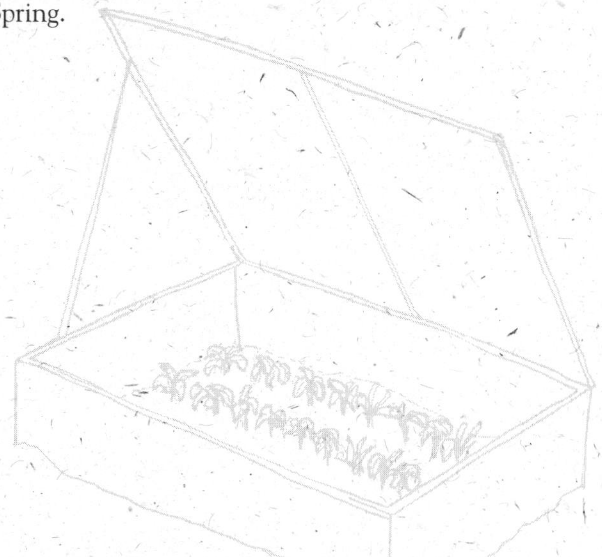

Notes

Spring Soup Tonics

Unlike the dreaded dose of strong-tasting Spring Tonic spooned into the family's mouths in Grandmother's day, a brothy Spring herb soup can be just as effective. Ladled into bowls at the family table this tonic is more likely to bring "Oliver" exclamations for "more"!

Fresh new tender nettle leaves or the greens of bolting chervil can be the herb of the country Spring soup, with cultivated dandelion or sorrel leaf for the city version.

For a **simple recipe**, cook 1/2C of organic whole oat groats (or 1/3C steel-cut/Irish oats) in a cup of water. Add 4C of vegetable broth (or 2 water + 2 broth) and heat to piping hot. Stir in 1 Tbs finely-grated fresh ginger root, juice and grated rind of 1/2 lemon, and a sizable bunch of one of the above Spring herbs, which have been swish-washed, drained and finely chopped. Toss in a handful of minced green onion, sprinkle with a bit of salt or stir in 3 Tbs light miso and serve immediately!

Tips for making vegetable broth or stock:

Like the witches brew from MacBeth, but infinitely richer in valuable minerals is a good organic broth. **Save** all those ends and stems from vegetables; wilted, NOT ROTTED green leaves; apple, pear cores (or other bits of fruits in season) and an occasional lemon rind or banana peel—be sure all ingredients are ORGANIC please!

They can be **collected and stored** for several days in a covered glass or crockery container in the refrigerator; then emptied into a large pot. (Add a bay leaf for flavor and/or fennel seeds if cabbage family vegetables are included.) Cover with water, bring to a boil over medium heat, and simmer on low for about 30 minutes. Set aside. When cool enough to handle, remove the cooked pulp with slotted spoon and discard or compost. **Ladle** the remaining golden or rosy broth through a sieve—lined with doubled, fine cheesecloth—into bottles or jars. The last few spoonsful in the bottom of the pot can be discarded if it contains sand or silt from the vegetables—though sterile from cooking, its grit is not a welcome addition in the soup bowl.

Cap, cool and refrigerate this **broth elixir** to use in soups, sauces, or serve with minced herb and salt as a first course.

Notes

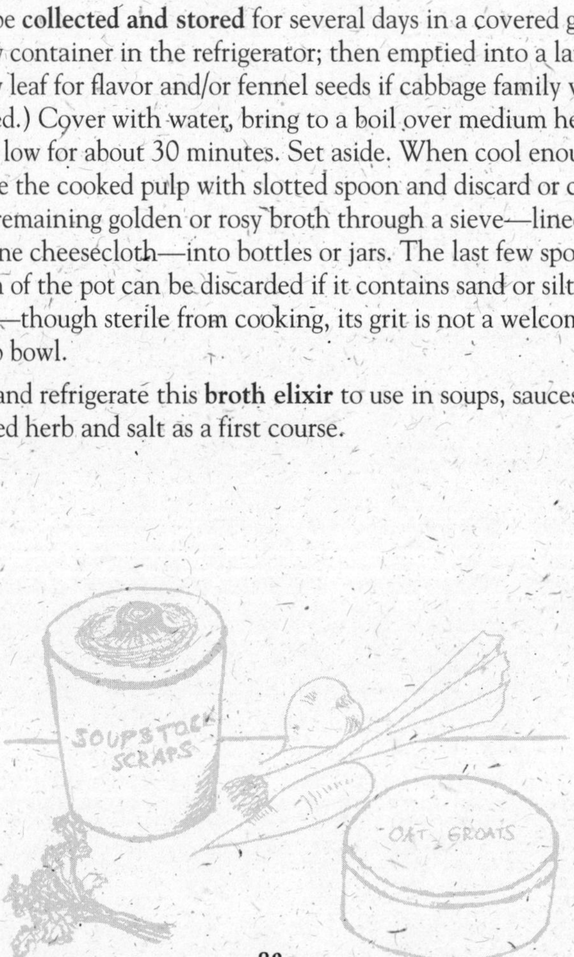

Index

Bold indicates primary information page.

Index *(Continued)*

Bold indicates primary information page.